The Maker's Mark

The Maker's Mark

*Exploring the Character of Jesus
Through the Fruit of the Spirit*

ANDY PERCEY

Foreword by Michael Card

WIPF & STOCK · Eugene, Oregon

THE MAKER'S MARK
Exploring the Character of Jesus Through the Fruit of the Spirit

Copyright © 2025 Andy Percey. All rights reserved. Except for brief quotations in critical publications or reviews, no part of this book may be reproduced in any manner without prior written permission from the publisher. Write: Permissions, Wipf and Stock Publishers, 199 W. 8th Ave., Suite 3, Eugene, OR 97401.

Wipf & Stock
An Imprint of Wipf and Stock Publishers
199 W. 8th Ave., Suite 3
Eugene, OR 97401

www.wipfandstock.com

PAPERBACK ISBN: 979-8-3852-4464-5
HARDCOVER ISBN: 979-8-3852-4465-2
EBOOK ISBN: 979-8-3852-4466-9

11/25/25

All Scripture unless otherwise stated is from the HOLY BIBLE, NEW INTERNATIONAL VERSION®, NIV® Copyright © 1973, 1978, 1984, 2011 by Biblica, Inc. Used with permission. All rights reserved worldwide.

Where noted, Scriptures are from *THE MESSAGE: The Bible in Contemporary Language* Copyright © 2002 by Eugene H. Peterson. All rights reserved.

Where noted, Scriptures are from the New King James Version®. Copyright © 1982 by Thomas Nelson. Used by permission. All rights reserved.

Where noted, Scriptures are from the *New Life Version*, Copyright © 1969 and 2003. Used by permission of Barbour Publishing, Inc., Uhrichsville, Ohio 44683. All rights reserved.

Where noted, Scripture quotations are from The Living Bible, copyright © 1971 by Tyndale House Foundation. Used by permission of Tyndale House Publishers, Carol Stream, Illinois 60188. All rights reserved.

For my parents, Sue and Brian

Thank you for planting the seeds of faith, love, and grace in my life.
Your example has shown me the character of Jesus
more clearly than words ever could.
I can't think of anyone whose character is more worthy
to dedicate a book on Godly character to than yours.

I love you both!

Contents

Foreword by Michael Card | ix

Preface | xi

Thanks | xiii

1   The Disconnect | 1

2   The Mark | 13

3   Love | 28

4   Joy | 44

5   Peace | 60

6   Patience | 78

7   Kindness | 93

8   Goodness | 109

9   Faithfulness | 123

10 Gentleness | 141

11 Self-Control | 159

12 A Life of Spirit-Formed Character | 177

Bibliography | 183

Foreword

When Paul met Gaius in Derbe, he received the troubling news. Things weren't going so well in the region of Galatia. The churches there were under attack from Judaizers, who were teaching the Gentiles that they had to convert to Judaism in order to become true Christians. They were twisting the gospel by demanding the proof of good works. The good news was rapidly becoming bad news.

Scholars, agree, this is Paul's angriest letter. He is defending his flock and his own reputation. In contrast to the false teaching that we are simply machines meant to crank out good news, Paul speaks in chapter 5 of a life that is called to bear fruit, a single fruit with nine dimensions: love, joy, peace, patience, kindness, goodness, faithfulness, gentleness and self-control.

Before the nine-fold positive list of the various aspects of the fruit of the Spirt, there is a much longer list of the "deeds of the flesh." There are fifteen of these: sexual immorality, impurity, indecent behavior, idolatry, witchcraft, hostilities, strife, jealousy, outbursts of anger, selfish ambition, dissensions, factions, envy, drunkenness, and carousing. One wonders if this list is related to the behavior of some of those in some of the Galatian churches and might explain some of the anger in Paul's response. Whatever the case, Paul moves on to the nine positive aspects of the fruit of the Spirit

It is the list we all memorized in Sunday school. The first person who could recite it correctly and in order would receive a prize. Unfortunately, many of us believed once the list was locked in our memory we were done with it. But the truth is, we are never done with it, and it is never done with us. It can be understood as a portrait of Jesus because these nine traits were perfectly incarnated in his life. The incarnation made them one.

Jesus deeply disliked fruitlessness. It is the cause of his two most angry outbursts. In Matthew 23 Jesus pronounces the "woes" upon the Pharisees. In one way or another all of the woes can be connected to the fruitless lives

Foreword

of the Pharisees. In an earlier and somewhat more mysterious incident, Jesus actually curses a fruitless fig tree. This unique moment happens in Mark 11 and Matthew 21. As he is entering Jerusalem for one of the last times he is hungry and spots a fig tree in leaf. When he comes to the tree he finds that it is barren, fruitless, and in his frustration pronounces a curse on the tree, that no one will ever eat fruit from it ever again. The mystery of this incident comes in the parenthetical statement that it was not the season of figs. Jesus, with his rural upbringing must have certainly know this. The mystery is solved when we realize that the incident is not really about the little barren tree at all. It is about the fruitlessness of Israel. The tree is merely a symbol. Paul's fifteen item list of the deeds of the flesh are embodied in this mysterious story. Jesus is angered when he is reminded by the fruitless tree of the fifteen effects of fruitlessness.

Paul almost certainly knew this story. It was surely a part of the traditions that had been circulated in the early church. Paul understood Jesus' anger in regards to fruitlessness. He had sensed it in the Galatian churches and, like Jesus, it angered him too. And so after the longer fruitless list, he provides the jewel that is the nine-fold list describing the qualities of the fruit of the Spirit. It is, in the end, a description of the life of Jesus, a portrait of what the fruit of his life was like.

The call of Galatians is for this fruit to be born in our lives as the spirit causes us to bear the image of Christ.

Andy is a pastor, and this book is pastoral in the best sense of the word. Certainly it is rooted in scripture, structured somewhat like a sermon. It points on every page to Jesus and behind each sentence is a pastor's heart.

Michael Card
Singer, Songwriter & Author

Preface

I WAS READING PSALM 139 recently, and verse 5 really struck me;

"You hem me in behind and before, and you lay your hand upon me."

It's the image of a Creator who is both close and intentional, a Maker who not only forms but also shapes, guides, and marks His creation with care. That line captures the heart of this book: not just that we are made by God, but that we are made as those who bear His mark.

Over the years, as a pastor, friend, and sometimes fumbling follower of Jesus, I've become increasingly aware that we live in a world that is often more interested in impressions than integrity and personality over character. We're coached in how to stand out, but rarely in how to stand firm. In the noise of constant connection, so many feel more disconnected than ever: from each other, from themselves, and, most painfully, from the One who made them.

This book is partly written in response to that ache. Not just my own, but the one I have seen mirrored in conversations with family, friends, and those I've walked with as a Pastor, discussed over many cups of coffee. It's for those of us who want to live lives that are more than polished performances. Who long to live with depth, with purpose, with character that reflects something, someone, greater.

The good news, the gospel truth, is that we were made to do just that. From the first breath of creation, God marked humanity with His image. Not as a stamp of status, but as a shaping of substance. That divine mark wasn't a symbol to display but a source to draw from, a code written into our souls, a reflection of the Maker Himself.

But life happens. And along the way, that mark becomes dulled, buried under the pressures of modern life, hidden beneath the layers of brokenness we all carry, distorted by the lies we've been told or started to

Preface

tell ourselves. We lose sight of who we are because we lose sight of *whose* we are.

Here is the great hope: the mark is never erased, and the call to reflect it hasn't changed.

What you hold in your hands is an invitation to recover that mark. Not through striving or self-improvement plans, but through returning. Returning to God. To the truth of who He is, and the truth of who you are because of Him. Through the life, death, and resurrection of Jesus, the mark of God; His character, His love, His Spirit, becomes not just something we bear, but something we *become*.

So, we'll begin with honesty; about the disconnects we feel. Then we'll journey through the fruit of the Spirit, not as virtues to tick off, but as glimpses of the kind of character that grows when we live rooted in Christ and shaped by the Spirit. This isn't about perfection. It's about presence. It's about pattern. It's about walking closely enough with Jesus that His character begins to show up in ours.

This won't always be easy. But it will be worth it. Because how we live in this world matters. And because you, dear reader, are fearfully and wonderfully made and you carry the Maker's mark.

Welcome to the journey.

Thanks

WRITING *THE MAKER'S MARK* has been a journey of reflection, prayer, and deep gratitude. This book would not exist without the faithfulness and encouragement of many people who have walked with me along the way.

First, to Jesus. The true image of the invisible God, the only one who bears the Maker's mark perfectly, and the one in whom all character finds its fullness. Thank You for your patience in shaping mine, for your grace when I fall, and for being the model I seek to follow every day.

To new friends at Wipf and Stock for making this book possible.

To Michael, for not only writing the foreword for this book, but for your many years of ministry bearing the Maker's mark, that have so blessed and shaped my faith.

To trusted friends Andy and Sharon, for your friendship, grace, and wisdom to make this a better book.

To my copyeditor Amanda, for all your hard work and skill to help shape and hone this work.

To by beautiful wife Bex, and our amazing son Leo. Thank you for being the ones to show me what Christ-like character looks like in real life. Your constant faith, quiet strength, and unconditional love have left a mark on me that words can hardly capture. Thank you for inspiring me to keep pushing deeper, and for all your wisdom at work in every page!

To my mentors and teachers, thank you for your wisdom, challenge, and example. You helped me see that formation is a lifelong process, and you gave me tools to keep growing.

To my friends and church family at Manvers Street Baptist Church, thank you for the conversations, prayers, and honest community that made these pages possible. As a Church at the Centre of Community, you inspire me that we grow best when we grow together.

To every reader who picks up this book... thank you!

Thanks

May it serve as both a mirror and a map, pointing you back to Jesus, the one who shapes us with gentleness and truth. I pray these words stir a deeper hunger in you to bear his image more fully in the world.

With gratitude and every blessing

Andy Percey
Summer, 2025

1

The Disconnect

"He's a bit of a character."
    When I am preparing to take a person's funeral, I like to meet with the family to learn more from them about their loved one, who they were, how they lived, what made them, *them*. Recently during such a visit, the family described their recently deceased father as "a bit of a character." Since that visit I've been thinking about what that means, because in many ways it is something very different to that concept of character that we are going to explore in this book. What they meant was that he was a man full of personality. You couldn't miss him, he stood out in a room, he was the life and soul of the party. Many of the stories the family shared, which I got to share with the hundreds that gathered to say goodbye to him, made me smile. Like the time he and his brother crawled into the heating grates in the floor of the local Abbey to collect the change that had fallen out of people's pockets!
    What this family were describing to me, through these stories and all that they shared, was something of the man's personality. It was the outward face that he showed to the world. If you were to describe friends or people you know, the odds are that you will describe something of their personality, what they are like or how they come across to you. But it's important not to mix up "character" and "personality" which our society uses interchangeably, because while there is overlap between the two, there are also significant differences. I won't go into these differences, but I mention it here to reinforce the importance of character over personality.

What character is can be hard to define, and our thinking will evolve as we go on this journey together. I think many of us would know what we mean when we use the word but would find it hard to give voice to what it looks like when it is lived out. We certainly know when we come across people of bad character.

Essentially though most psychologists agree that character is what shapes us. It is those beliefs and values that give meaning to everything we do. It is the "code" that we live by, directing our actions and the shape of our lives. It is *who* we are. Not only does our character shape us but it can also be shaped. I'm going to expand on that a little as we go on, but as we begin, I want us to be aware of some challenges we face as we seek to grow in this critical area of discipleship.

THE MAKER'S MARK

I feel blessed that in growing up I had countless positive role models. I had godly women and men who I could look up to, whose shoulders I stood upon, and who's example I still try to follow. Some are found within my family. Others within the church. Some more widely. Their faith was invitational. They shared time, wisdom, and comfort with me. They looked beyond the worst or most broken parts of me and saw that transformational work could take place.

Time spent with them was rich and rarely rushed and I am forever grateful for their example. They are people of character.

Who are those character role models for you?

Sadly, I talk to people all the time in my role as a pastor who never had that example growing up. They desperately looked for it, and in not finding it around them, looked further and further afield to find it. The problem was that the more they looked the harder the search became, leading to greater feelings of despondency and a greater risk that people looked in the wrong places.

The word "character" comes from a Greek word for an "engraved mark." When the metalsmith, writer, artist, or inventor puts their mark of ownership on a piece, that is a character mark. It not only identifies who made it but is a guarantee of the quality of the piece and its accurate reflection of its creator.

When God makes us in his image, it is a character mark, a mark of creatorship that is imprinted onto our very souls that tells us who we were made by, our quality and our reflection of our maker. That is what we see in creation in Genesis, but we see it reflected so beautifully in the Psalms too:

> "For you created my inmost being;
>   you knit me together in my mother's womb.
> I praise you because I am fearfully and wonderfully made;
>   your works are wonderful,
>   I know that full well."[1]

That we are made "good," in the image of God, to reflect who he is in his world is meant to inform the essence of who we are. It is the code we are to live by, the image we are called to reflect, and our behaviors and personality traits healthily flow from that reality.

There are two truths that exist in our lives that inform how we live. We find them at the moment of creation all the way back in Genesis:

> "So God created mankind in his own image,
>   in the image of God he created them;
>   male and female he created them."[2]

And then a few verses later:

> "God saw all that he had made, and it was very good . . ."[3]

This is the truth from the very beginning, that God made us as good, and as those who would live and reflect his image in the world he created. We are God's good image bearers. That is what should shape us and give meaning to all we do. It is what gives shape to our lives. It is who we are.

Those family members and friends that I admired and looked up to growing up, and those I do today, are those in whom I see the Maker's mark clearly. Not only that, but they are those who by their very nature affirm that in me too.

Are they perfect? No. Am I perfect? No!! That too is a reality we need to acknowledge in our quest to live with godly character.

Paul puts it with characteristic brutal honesty:

> "for all have sinned and fall short of the glory of God . . ."[4]

---

1. Ps 139:13–14.
2. Gen 1:27.
3. Gen 1:31.
4. Rom 3:23.

That beautiful divine mark we have been adorned with became covered up. Like dirt and grease can hide a mark on beautiful metal, so the dirt and grime of our own rebelliousness can hide and cover that mark in our own lives. We become disconnected from the reality of who we are, as our true self is covered over by layer and layer of bad choices and broken thinking.

Part of the reason why we recognize bad character in the world is that we know it all too well in our own lives. There is an old saying which says, "the pathway to hell is paved with good intentions." This doesn't mean that we should give up trying to live well, or right with God, but it highlights that intentions themselves aren't enough. Just wanting to be better or even trying to be better isn't enough for us. As Paul wrote to the Romans:

> "Yes. I'm full of myself—after all, I've spent a long time in sin's prison. What I don't understand about myself is that I decide one way, but then I act another, doing things I absolutely despise. So if I can't be trusted to figure out what is best for myself and then do it, it becomes obvious that God's command is necessary.
>
> But I need something more! For if I know the law but still can't keep it, and if the power of sin within me keeps sabotaging my best intentions, I obviously need help! I realize that I don't have what it takes. I can will it, but I can't do it. I decide to do good, but I don't really do it; I decide not to do bad, but then I do it anyway. My decisions, such as they are, don't result in actions. Something has gone wrong deep within me and gets the better of me every time."[5]

Who we are as God's good image bearers has been distorted and covered to such a degree that even our own intentions let us down, and as Peterson translates Pauls' words here, "I need something more." We cannot do it on our own. We cannot rediscover the paradise that was lost, we cannot uncover the Maker's mark.

This is the reality that Paul lived within, and so do we. We live out of an intention planted deep with us to live as we were created to live; but sin corrupts and gets in the way, an unending cycle of trial and error, of two steps forward and three steps backwards. Something needs to change, and it cannot be changed by you and me.

---

5. Rom 7:15–20, *Message*.

DISCONNECTED AND ISOLATED LIVES

We will explore later how this cycle is broken, and what that means for us as we seek to live lives reflecting the character of Jesus. For now, I want us to explore the outcome of that cycle, and how we often do try to "work on it" ourselves.

I saw a video on social media recently that both made me laugh and hit home a little too much. The video highlighted the difference between our attitude and behavior when we are walking and when we are driving. While walking, the man is polite, courteous and considerate. He gives way to others and is apologetic when needed. It stands in stark contrast to the section when he is driving. He is rushed and rude. He swears. He complains if a person is driving 10 miles an hour under the speed limit in front of him. He gets cross if someone doesn't say thank you to him when he lets them out at a junction.

What hits home about the video is that it highlights the inconsistency in how we live. We behave one way in one setting, and totally different in another. This isn't just isolated to when we are in the car, but we see it across multiple areas of our lives. We can be different at work to how we are at home. We can be different with our friends to how we are with our family. We can be one thing to one person, and someone totally different with another. Don't get me wrong, there are times when this is natural and necessary. You don't behave the same way with your kids as you do with your boss. How you express who you are with your spouse will be different to how you express yourself with your friends. But when that is done healthily, when living out of our God given character, there is a consistency even within the difference.

Do you see any inconsistency in your life? How many versions of you are there? Is the "real" you, created as good in the image of God, still visible?

I don't want to highlight the inconsistencies to make us feel discouraged, but to recognize that being people of character is a challenge, and we don't always have great role models. When we look around us, whether it is in the world of politics, of social media, or celebrity culture, we notice a lack of genuine good character. We live in a culture where personality is king and where popular characteristics trump character. We live in a world where people promise much, presenting the most appealing version of themselves to whomever happens to be in front of them. This isn't just isolated to political debating chambers or Instagram posts, but we see it all around us. In our workplaces, in our homes and families, and within our own individual lives.

It can be easy for us to become stamped with other marks of ownership; popularity, success, and happiness, and for the pursuit of those things to drive us. The challenge here is that, when we are marked by and chase after something other than God, then we will become whatever we need to be to get it. When we are marked by "success," then the danger is that we will do whatever we need to do to be successful. When we are marked by "popularity," then the danger is that we will do whatever it takes to be popular. In one of my previous books, *Made to Belong*, I told a story of a conversation between my friend Jon and I as a teenager. My friend called me out on not really knowing the real me. We need friends like that who know us well enough to see when we are living inconsistently, and honest enough with us to point that out. As we read in Proverbs:

"Wounds from a friend can be trusted . . ."[6]

Who are the friends in your life who know you well enough to keep you living authentically and consistently as the person God has made you? You need to make yourself accountable, ask someone to fulfil that role in your life. It won't always be easy, in fact there will be times when it is painful, but it will be worth it; those wounds can be trusted.

The great challenge is the desire to try and "work on ourselves" in isolation. Firstly, and this is something we will go on to explore in more detail as we journey together, the concept of "working on myself" is unhelpful. It ticks a couple of boxes that makes us feel good about ourselves; it sounds productive, and it remains private; but it misses the heart of character, which is that it flows from living as those marked by God as his. It also misses the mark because our living this out was never meant to be in isolation. Think back to the Genesis text we explored a moment ago. God made *them* in his image. We were not meant to do it alone. In fact, the first instance we see of a human being on their own was when temptation slipped in, and the enemy sold the lie that would threaten to drive a wedge between God and his creation forever. When we isolate ourselves, it is easier to believe the lies of the enemy, lies about who we are and lies about God.

This journey of consistent living requires others to walk it with us. It requires the encouragement of a great cloud of witness so that we might

---

6. Prov 27:6.

"throw off everything that hinders and the sin that so easily entangles. And let us run with perseverance the race marked out for us . . . "[7]

Not only the fellowship of a great crowd, but also the intimate and vulnerable companionship of accountability. If we really want to grow as people of character, then we need others.

There are those who will serve as a model to us, great women and men of faith to look up to, whose lives of consistent character will be a great example to us. But as we have already seen, we also live in a world where there are those who will serve as a warning to us. The inconsistency of their lives may win short term friends but never foster long term relationships. They might be real *characters*, but they lack *real* character.

THE SHADOW SIDE

Another danger of living in an isolated life is that we can develop shadow sides.

We live in a big world, and it sometimes helps to compartmentalize our lives, but the danger there is that we can end up compartmentalizing our souls. We all have areas of our lives that we aren't aware of; emotions or desires that we haven't given conscious acknowledgement of. A side that feels darker or more chaotic? Messy maybe?

Each of us has these areas in our lives, but part of the importance of living with consistent character is that we allow light to shine into these areas of ourselves, rather than keeping them hidden.

It might be that shame takes hold, and that is a cause of keeping something hidden. Think back again to the when Adam and Eve first stepped away from living as those made in the image of God. What was the result:

> "Then the eyes of both of them were opened, and they realized they were naked; so they sewed fig leaves together and made coverings for themselves.
>
> Then the man and his wife heard the sound of the Lord God as he was walking in the garden in the cool of the day, and they hid from the Lord God among the trees of the garden. But the Lord God called to the man, "Where are you?"
>
> He answered, "I heard you in the garden, and I was afraid because I was naked; so I hid."[8]

7. Heb 12:1.
8. Gen 3:7–10.

The Maker's Mark

They were ashamed, so they hid. How often do we do the same? When we feel ashamed of something we have done, we hide. Hide from others, hide from ourselves, and hide from God. Rather than allow the light of his presence to bring us healing and wholeness, we prefer to sit in the little dark corners of our souls until eventually we make our home in them.

What we need is light. Within the first couple of verses in the Bible we see not only God's creative expression, but through it, the light that we need:

> "Now the earth was formless and empty, darkness was over the surface of the deep, and the Spirit of God was hovering over the waters.
> And God said, "Let there be light," and there was light."[9]

There was darkness and emptiness, but God filled it up with light. Into the chaos of formless nothingness God brought order, and he's been doing it repeatedly since the beginning. We see it most clearly and fully not through the sun that shines down it's light and heat upon our world, but in the giving of God's own son:

> "In him was life, and that life was the light of all people. The light shines in the darkness, and the darkness has not put it out."[10]

The light that Jesus brought into the world is one that the darkness cannot stand. Not only is it incapable of putting it out, but it flees in the face of it, like how darkness disappears from a room when you turn on a light.

That is what we need in those dark and isolated places of our hearts and souls. Light. The light of God to shine in all its creative and chaos-banishing brilliance. There will be times when that illumination is painful and brings to light things that we would feel more comfortable with being hidden; but that light always brings order to the chaos. It allows creation to take place.

We need to be honest with ourselves. Because without that honesty there is denial, and there can be no change when we live in denial.

Brian McLaren speaks in his book *Naked Spirituality* about how C.S. Lewis would ask "what is the most important conversation you have every day?"

"People would respond piously, "your conversation with God, of course." "No," Lewis would reply. "It is the conversation you have with

9. Gen 1:2–3.
10. John 1:4–5.

yourself before you speak to God, because in that conversation with yourself, you decide whether you are going to be honest and authentic with God, or whether you are going to meet him with a false face, a mask, an act, a pretense."[11]

When we come to God in prayer, we rarely need our arms twisting to bring to him our requests for what we need. Or even our requests for others. What we do not always do is share with honesty who we are, holding ourselves before the Lord in that moment with naked vulnerability. We might fool ourselves in thinking that he knows anyway, so why all this need for "naval gazing?" Of course he knows. Do we really think that he couldn't find Adam and Eve in the garden? He knew where they were, but he still called for them. The Lord knows what is going on in the deepest darkest parts of our lives too, to a greater degree than we can even know. And yet he still calls out to you, longing that you would be open and honest with him, because when you do you open channels in the darkness for his light to come in.

John writes in the first of his later letters:

> "This is the message we have heard from him and declare to you: God is light; in him there is no darkness at all. If we claim to have fellowship with him and yet walk in the darkness, we lie and do not live out the truth. But if we walk in the light, as he is in the light, we have fellowship with one another, and the blood of Jesus, his Son, purifies us from all sin."[12]

If you light a candle in a dark room, and then you shine a torch onto it to cast a shadow on the wall you will notice that you can only see the candlestick itself. The flame, the light, casts no shadow. God is light—the total absence of darkness; and as those who are made in his image, who bear his mark, we are called to walk in that light. As Charles Wesley wrote in his well-loved hymn "And Can It Be":

> Long my imprisoned spirit lay
> Fast bound in sin and nature's night;
> Thine eye diffused a quickening ray,
> I woke, the dungeon flamed with light;
> My chains fell off, my heart was free;
> I rose, went forth and followed Thee.[13]

11. McLaren, *Naked Spirituality*, 111.
12. 1 John 1:5–7.
13. Charles Wesley, "And Can It Be" (1738).

The Maker's Mark

There is no place too dark that the light of Jesus cannot break in. There is no part of your past so broken that the Lord cannot bring his healing. There is no shame you feel too weighty that he cannot free you from its burden. There is no prison you feel trapped in that he cannot break the bars of and bring release. If you feel broken, shamed, imprisoned or trapped in darkness today, may you know these words from Zachariah's song to be true for you.

> Because the heart of our God is full of loving-kindness for us, a light from heaven will shine on us. It will give light to those who live in darkness and are under the shadow of death. It will lead our feet in the way of peace.[14]

HOW WE LIVE MATTERS

Why does all this matter? Because you do! So does how you live in this world. We often search around us for the direction our lives should take, from the more immediate "how should I fill my day," to the larger "where is my life going" questions. We want to have lives that are full of purpose and meaning which brings with it the fulfilment we long to see.

We look for that, and if we cannot find it with ourselves as the people that God has created us to be then we will go searching for it in other places.

We are constantly bombarded with messages and images about who we are, what shape our lives should take, our values etc. Social media gives us a fake picture of what our lives should be, broken down into hundreds of choreographed moments that will paint the picture of perfect lives. How are we as Christians meant to live in this world, and not just survive in it, but to thrive and live authentically and uncompromisingly for Jesus?

How you live in this world matters. It matters because we see far too often Christians who live one way in church and then totally differently in the world. It matters, because as you bear the creators mark into the world, you are an ambassador of his Kingdom.

In Exodus 20 we see the list of Commandments that God gave to his people at the mountain. The third commandment we often translate as this:

> "Do not take the name of the LORD your God in vain."[15]

---

14. Luke 1:78–79.
15. Exod 20:7.

Our takeaway from this verse is usually that we aren't allowed to say the phrase "Oh my God." In our family we don't use that phrase. However, there is so much more to it than that, and the command is far more radical than many of us think.

We could translate the verse equally as this:

> "Do not carry the name of the LORD your God as nothing."

There is a real difference here! Rather than just avoiding saying one phrase, this is about how we live in the world as those who carry the name of Jesus. Do we live in such a way that those who look on at our lives of faith see nothing of Jesus? Because we can avoid saying "OMG" our whole lives long, but if we do not carry the name of Jesus in our lives in a way that means something, then we have misunderstood the commandment.

Having Godly character also gives us healthy relationships, which is one of the aspects of life that God has created us to enjoy, and which gives life so much of its meaning. Throughout this book we will look at the specifics of Jesus-shaped character by exploring the fruit of the Spirit, looking at how the presence of this fruit enriches our relationships deeply.

Imagine what a difference your life would make to those around you if you lived reflecting the image of God. How would your marriage or your relationship with your children look? How would it bless your friends and neighbors? Would it make a difference to the culture of your workplace?

How we live in the world matters. We should live within it but not be filled with it.

Paul warns us not to "become so well-adjusted to your culture that you fit into it without even thinking."[16]

A ship sails on the water, but if it gets filled with water then it sinks. The same is true for us as those who follow Jesus; we live in this world, but if we become filled with it, with its priorities, values, and character, then we too will sink.

Yes, there is tremendous challenge here. Living for Jesus is not easy. Growing in character is not easy. However, paying attention to your spiritual walk and character growth is one of the most important things that you will ever do, and it will make significant changes in your life and the lives of the people around you.

---

16. Rom 12:2, *Message*.

As we begin this journey together, despite the challenges, we have every reason to hope because built into us from the very beginning is the reality that we are "good" and created in the image of God.

We bear the Maker's mark.

QUESTIONS FOR REFLECTION

1. Who are the role models you look up to?
2. What in your life has "marked" you?
3. How consistent is your life?
4. Are there areas of your life where you need the shadow-banishing light of God to shine?
5. How honest are you prepared to be with God?
6. How are you carrying the name of the LORD in your life?

2

The Mark

SOME OF YOU MIGHT remember the TV show *Stars in their Eyes*, a popular show when I was growing up where ordinary people came on to be dressed up and perform like their musical heroes. The famous line as they disappeared through the screens before being revealed to the waiting audience was "tonight, Matthew, I'm going to be . . . " Cue the makeup and costume teams, and with a little bit of clever TV editing, Julian the postal worker was transformed into Elton John. We all want to look like our heroes.

We have explored the challenges in growing as people of character, but we all need people around us who will model, in positive ways, what good character looks like. We have already given thanks for those people in our lives who have lived out their faith in beautiful ways, and now we are going to explore a little more of how our character should be shaped. Or rather, in whose image it is shaped.

CONFORMED INTO THE LIKENESS OF HIS SON

Paul writes to the Romans:

> "For those God foreknew he also predestined to be conformed to the image of his Son . . . "[1]

Whenever I have had discussions around the meaning of this verse, they have usually been heavy ones that focus on the meaning of the word

---

1. Rom 8:29.

"predestined." It's a discussion or debate that does the rounds in every generation, and usually focusses on who's *in* and who's *out*, and what choice we have in the matter. Over the years I have landed on both sides of the discussion, but now find myself wondering, at times sadly, whether we have missed the point of what Paul teaches us here. Eugene Peterson helpfully translates this section of Romans 8 in this way:

> "God knew what he was doing from the very beginning. He decided from the outset to shape the lives of those who love him along the same lines as the life of his Son. The Son stands first in the line of humanity he restored. We see the original and intended shape of our lives there in him."[2]

What is your life shaped on? What are the goals, destinations, and people that you line your life up with? Every one of us has goals, things we want to achieve in life, people that we look up to and want to emulate. What are yours?

For Paul the goal, destination, or to use a popular word today, the *destiny* of all those who come to faith is that they become more like Jesus. As much as we want to look up to those around us, our pastors or leaders, family and friends, figures in public life, or even the heroes of faith from scripture; if you are a Christian today then, as far as Paul believed, the focus and direction of your life is that you look more like Jesus. That's who your life is lined up to.

That's a big ask. Being like Jesus! We tend to aim lower and emulate those around us because that feels more achievable. After all, we take great comfort from the fact that the greats of our faith made huge mistakes. That makes us feel better about ourselves. Jesus feels far too beyond our reach; he is the Son of God after all.

We focus so much on the divinity of Jesus in order that we might worship him, that we have lost something of his humanity. After all, when he healed the sick, raised the dead, taught the most profound teaching of any age, that was God wasn't it? If we think that, then we relegate the humanity of Jesus as simply being the legs that carried God around the countryside. And it means that Jesus seems even further from our humanity than we have ever thought. We think, "it can't have been all that hard being human when you spoke the stars into being?!" As John Eldredge puts it in his book *Beautiful Outlaw*, it's like:

---

2. Rom 8:29–30, *Message*.

> "Einstein has dropped in to take the 1st grade Math quiz. Mozart is playing a measure in the kindergarten song flute choir."[3]

It's easy for God to play at being human. That's the accusation. You won't find that in the gospels though, written by the people who spent time living with Jesus as he traveled around the countryside. The Word becomes flesh[4] according to John and lived among us; but he did so embracing our humanity, laying aside the rights and privileges of heaven to become one of us. He wasn't God playing a human like some sort of human being in *cheat mode*. He was fully one of us, and that is the great and profound mystery of the incarnation. He was, and is, the only one to ever be fully both. We have no frame of reference for him. He stands in the long line of human beings who have and will ever live, completely unique.

I remember a well-respected tutor in Bible College saying that it was not hard to say that Jesus was fully God and fully human. The challenge was to say that he was fully God without prejudice to him being fully human; and fully human without prejudice to him being fully God. In other words, Jesus didn't cheat!

I recently played golf with some friends, and on one hole there was a steep walk uphill. About halfway up I was struggling and lamenting my apparent lack of fitness. I was surprised though that I was *that* unfit and that as my friends were strolling purposely forwards, I was falling behind. Then, three quarters of the way up the hill I identified my problem; both to my horror and relief, my golf trolley still had the brake on!

Jesus shows us what humanity without the brakes on looks like, striding purposely forwards up the hill that we struggle with because sin and brokenness so often choke our progress.

In Jesus we see what true humanity is really like. True humanity made alive in the Spirit of God. True humanity bearing the Maker's mark. True and good humanity living in the image of God. As the writer of Hebrews begins his letter:

> "The Son is the radiance of God's glory and the exact representation of his being . . ."[5]

When we look to Jesus, we see who God fully is, but we also see what humanity really is too.

3. Eldredge, *Beautiful Outlaw*, 44.
4. John 1:14.
5. Heb 1:3.

The Maker's Mark

Brennan Manning reminds us:

> "He is a man in a way we had forgotten men can be: truthful, blunt, emotional, nonmanipulative, sensitive, compassionate."[6]

So, when we are shaped into the image of Jesus we begin to experience what real humanity is. In dying to myself and my own priorities and values I can begin to reflect the image of the One who is most fully and authentically human. I wonder, when people look at our churches, do they see human beings at their best? At their most loving and tender, gracious and compassionate, just and protective, truthful and sensitive? Beyond the songs, prayers and programs do they catch a glimpse of something dangerously attractive, because it stokes a fire lit within us long ago to live as those who bear the Maker's mark?

This doesn't happen by accident, and it isn't some sort of behavior modification plan. You can't *make* yourself more like Jesus, or at least not on your own. What was that phrase that Paul used . . . *to be conformed*.

It is a process. It is not about information but about transformation. When I come to Jesus, I am made new, I can say with Paul "I am a new creation,"[7] but I am also in the process of being changed, renewed, and conformed into his likeness.

Sometimes we think that coming to faith is simply crossing a line; job done; I can simply get on with living the Chrisitan life carefree because I'm now *in*.

Yes, as Paul goes on to say in 2 Corinthians 5:17, "*the old has gone, the new is come,*" but that doesn't mean that we don't need to give attention to our spiritual development. That doesn't mean that the journey has finished. That doesn't mean that we aren't in need of constant transformation. If we ask ourselves the question, can I become more like Jesus, and the answer is *yes* (which for all of us it will be), then we have more in us to be transformed. When you are adopted into a family, the reality of adoption is only one part of the process. You also need to learn to live as part of that family, to grow into it, to develop relationships with others around you. That takes time, intention, and support.

Brennan Manning helpfully highlights this for us:

---

6. Manning, *Abba's Child*, 89.

7. 2 Cor 5:17.

> "For a disciple of Jesus the process of spiritual growth is a gradual repudiation of the unreal image of God . . ."[8]

God made people in his own image, and we have been returning the favor ever since. The problem when we make God in our own image is that our view of God is so small and limited that we can never really experience the transformation we need. Not from *that* God, made in *our* image.

Part of this journey of transformation is re-discovering who God really is, and rediscovering who we really are. Both are found in the person of Jesus. If I have made God in my own image; sometimes I might fool myself into thinking that it's because I am like him, but more often than I would like to admit it is because I have made him like me. Jesus comes to shatter God made in my image and instead show me who God really is. At the same time, he comes to strip away all the layers I have added onto the *me* God created me to be; all of the false identity, the shame and guilt, the things others have put on me; until what is left is a truer reflection of the true humanity he so fully embodies. You see we think that when it comes to transformation it starts with us, but this is about who God is long before it is ever about who we are.

As Brennan says in the above quote, this is a gradual process. It takes a lifetime, and that's what can often frustrate us. Why can't we just get zapped to end up as the finished product? Why does it take so long? In answer to that, it takes all the time you have. It is a life work brought about in you by the Holy Spirit. When Paul speaks to the Corinthians about the glory of God he gives them the image of Moses climbing the mountain. Being in the presence of God was so transformative for Moses that his face glowed when he came back down the mountain. Over time though, time away from the presence, that glow faded. He had to hide his face behind a veil so that they didn't notice. Paul then shifts his attention to us:

> "And all of us, with unveiled faces, seeing the glory of the Lord as though reflected in a mirror, are being transformed into the same image from one degree of glory to another; for this comes from the Lord, the Spirit."[9]

One degree at a time. When you think of a circle as 360°, our transformation is 1° at a time. That might seem slow, but it is genuine change that is brought about by the Spirit at work in our hearts and lives, uncovering the reality of

---

8. Manning, *Relentless Tenderness of Jesus*, 18.
9. 2 Cor 3:18.

who we are as made in the image of God. Moses removed the veil, and the glory faded away. In us the Spirit removes the veil of brokenness in our lives, and we are transformed little by little into the glorious likeness of Jesus.

As you think about change in your own life, it might be that you feel the pace of change is slow. Years may have passed, and you still might not have arrived at who you want to be. It might be that you are struggling with a particular issue for a long time, and it doesn't feel as though change is coming. But be encouraged that change can and will happen when we come to Jesus, but it might not be as fast as we would like it.

The Lord knows what in us needs the most urgent work and what change can wait. It might be the issue you identify as the most pressing area of your life isn't what the Lord thinks. He may identify a totally different area that needs working and that is where we need to trust him.

Either way, that work of transformation, of shaping us along the same lines as Jesus, has begun. We are not today who we once were, and God willing in the future we will not be who we are now. Looking like Jesus is our destiny, and as Paul confidently reminds the Philippians:

> "He who began a good work in you will carry it on to completion..."[10]

AN APPRENTICE OF THE KINGDOM AND THE KING

We aren't just called to be like Jesus in our nature, but to be like Jesus in what we do and how we live. Who we are fundamentally affects the way we live in the world. There may be specific tasks or roles that God has called you to, unique to the gifts he has given you and specific to the context you're in; but the mission of every disciple in every place is to carry on the ministry of Jesus in the power of the Holy Spirit.

In our church I recently spent over a year preaching through Luke's gospel on Sunday mornings because I wanted us as a church to be people who made our home in the gospels. If our mission is to carry on the ministry of Jesus in the power of the Holy Spirit, then we need two things to do that.

Firstly, we need to know what the ministry of Jesus was, and we cannot do that unless we spend time in the gospels.

Have you ever made a journey with others "in convoy" where you are following another car? Navigating traffic lights, roundabouts, junctions, and traffic can be a stressful experience, and you know that to arrive at the

---

10. Phil 1:6.

destination you need to keep a close eye on the one you are following. If you lose sight of them, you're lost.

We need to keep our eyes fixed on Jesus. As we wind through the roads and junctions of life, we need to make sure that we don't lose sight of him. We need to see Jesus, to be challenged and confronted by him, changed and transformed by him, and to learn at his feet along with the disciples for us to know what his ministry is all about, and then be able to go about that ministry ourselves.

The word disciple is not just the name given to the twelve men who Jesus chose to follow him. It is a name that predates the calling of the twelve and means follower or student. If you followed a Rabbi in first century Judea then you were that Rabbi's student, or disciple. So, if we are to follow Jesus today, not simply believe in him but really follow him, then we ourselves are disciples, and we stand in a long line of disciples. The very reason that any of us are followers of Jesus is because of the disciples who came before us, and we are called to make the disciples who will come after us. Rabbi Evan Moffic is his book about the Jewishness of Jesus, writes this about discipleship:

> "Rabbi Jesus understood that a disciple is more than a follower. A disciple is more than a student. A disciple is a link between the past, present and future. Without disciples we do not live on."[11]

The wonderful thing about this model of discipleship is that we are not alone. There are fellow disciples, pilgrim companions on that road with us. As I mentioned in the last chapter, to live consistently we need others around us, the great cloud of witnesses past, present and future to cheer us on. But our focus shouldn't be on the crowd, as the writer of Hebrews goes on to remind us:

> " . . . fixing our eyes on Jesus, the pioneer and perfecter of faith."[12]

As I have already touched on, the challenge for us is that when we take our eyes off Jesus and start to base our lives along other lines, or other people, then we lose sight of the best that God has for us. Social media has made the term "following" popular again, but this question is one of the most profound we can ask ourselves today—*who am I following?* Not on social

---

11. Moffic, *What Every Christian Needs to Know about the Jewishness of Jesus,* 62.
12. Heb 12:2a.

The Maker's Mark

media, but who am I basing the shape of my life on, who am I lining my life, goals and priorities up with?

The followers of Jesus in the early church did not primarily refer to themselves as *Christians*. That was a term that was given to them by the people of Antioch.[13] Even though the name has stuck and is the term most people around the world use for those who follow Jesus, it is a term that only appears three time in the scriptures.[14] The term that they seem to have self-identified as in those early years is "followers of the Way."[15] This reference to *the Way* was far more than a philosophical or theological position, and it was far more than a statement of who was *in* or *out*. It was the identity of discipleship that rooted itself in being like the rabbi you followed; it was a binding yourself to the one who said, "I am the Way, the truth and the life."[16]

Sadly, we often narrow the meaning of this statement of Jesus to mean that Jesus is the way of avoiding Hell and getting into Heaven. I remember going for an interview at a church many years ago where we were asked a question specifically about whether we would be preaching "hellfire and brimstone." I suspect that the person asking wasn't so much asking a genuine question, more than trying to find out if we would tick the same box he ticked. We didn't. It's not that I don't think there is a place to talk about hell in the pulpit, (because I think you can talk about anything), it's just that Jesus didn't talk a lot about it. There are half a dozen situations where Jesus mentions it, a couple of times in his teaching on the sermon on the mount in Matthew and Mark, and in criticism of the Pharisees. Hell is only mentioned once in the gospel of Luke and not at all in the whole of the gospel of John. What we see throughout the gospels though is an invitation to life; real, full and lasting life that Jesus comes to bring. As John Eldredge puts it so beautifully:

> "The word I choose to describe Jesus is Life. Pure, lush, exuberant Life. Life that proves to be unquenchable, unstoppable, indestructible."[17]

Yes, in choosing life I am being rescued from death, but Jesus as the Way, truth and life is so much more than escaping hell but a means through

---

13. See Acts 11:26.
14. See Acts 11:26, Acts 26:28, 1 Pet 4:12.
15. See Acts 9:1–2, Acts 19:9, Acts 19:23, Acts 22:4, Acts 24:14, Acts 24:22.
16. John 14:6.
17. Eldredge, *Beautiful Outlaw*, 198.

which we can be transformed into his likeness and making an impact on the world. John Mark Comer helpfully breaks it down for us by saying that the three goals of an apprentice/disciple are to be with your Rabbi, become like your Rabbi and to do as your Rabbi did.[18]

After all, the call of Jesus to those first disciples was simple and yet contained profound and life changing implications: "Come, follow me."

Being a disciple, an apprentice of the King is all about being shaped, little by little, by one degree of glory to the next into the image and likeness of Jesus. That is your destiny. Committing to that is a long journey, one that Eugene Peterson beautifully described as *a long obedience in the same direction*,[19] where my life becomes orientated to Jesus and bears his mark.

To carry on the ministry of Jesus in the power of the Holy Spirit we need to not only know about Jesus and his ministry, but secondly, we need to live in the power of the Holy Spirit.

When Jesus is preparing his disciples for his death and eventual return to heaven, he says this:

> "But very truly I tell you, it is for your good that I am going away. Unless I go away, the Advocate will not come to you; but if I go, I will send him to you."

After three years of living with Jesus, sharing with him, being taught by him and experiencing the miracles and the teaching, it must have seemed unimaginable to the disciples that it would be a good thing that Jesus was going away. It must have been heart-breaking. Jesus explains though, that for them to be the people he has chosen them to be, for them to carry on the ministry he has inducted them into, the Spirit needs to come.

The Twentieth century pastor and author A.W Tozer once said that if the Holy Spirit had been removed from the early church, then 90 percent of what they did would have stopped, and everyone would have noticed. He continued that if the Holy Spirit were removed from the church today then 90 percent of what we did would carry on anyway, and nobody would have noticed the difference.

We cannot live for Jesus today without the empowering of the Holy Spirit. We cannot hope to have character shaped like Jesus, to become more like him without the empowering of the Holy Spirit. There are times when we are so desperate to be about the work of the Kingdom that we

---

18. See Comer, *Practicing the Way*.
19. Peterson, *Long Obedience in the Same Direction*.

forget we are called to be apprentices of the King. We want to go, but there may be times when we are called to wait and receive the transformative anointing of the Spirit. We see that as the gospel of Matthew merges into the beginning of Acts.

> "Then Jesus came to them and said, 'All authority in heaven and on earth has been given to me. Therefore go and make disciples of all nations, baptizing them in the name of the Father and of the Son and of the Holy Spirit, and teaching them to obey everything I have commanded you. And surely I am with you always, to the very end of the age.'"[20]

Go . . . There is something about that word that many of us like, because it requires us to do something. It gives us something to work on, something to contribute to. It's active and by its very nature it requires us to do something.

But having told the disciples to go at the end of Matthew's gospel, we then hear the words of Jesus at the beginning of Acts:

> "On one occasion, while he was eating with them, he gave them this command: 'Do not leave Jerusalem, but *wait* for the gift my Father promised, which you have heard me speak about. For John baptized with water, but in a few days you will be baptized with the Holy Spirit.'"[21]

Wait . . . There is something about those words that is a challenge to many of us, because it seems so passive. There is nothing we can *do*.

Even here in these last moments before his ascension Jesus was teaching them. He was teaching them that for them to fulfil the great commission they will need help. That for them to carry on his ministry they were going to need help. That to be a people who were like him, who did what he did, who bore his mark in the world, they were going to need help and God himself was going to provide that help. It was a help that he had promised them weeks before:

> "The Advocate, the Holy Spirit, whom the Father will send in my name, will teach you all things and will remind you of everything I have said to you."[22]

---

20. Matt 28:18–20.
21. Acts 1:4–5.
22. John 14:26.

God is the God who gives himself: we see that with the coming of Jesus and we see it with the coming of the Holy Spirit.

The reason why the Spirit is so vital in carry on the ministry of Jesus is given to the disciples by Jesus himself:

> "And I will ask the Father, and he will give you *another* advocate to help you and be with you for ever – the Spirit of truth."[23]

It's worth reflecting on this word "another." There are two Greek words we translate into our English word *another*; ἕτερος which means, *another that is different*, and ἄλλον which means, *another that is the same*. Think of it like this, if you didn't like your shoes you might say, 'I don't like these shoes, I'm going to get another pair.' That would be ἕτερος. However, if you really liked your shoes you might say, "I really love my shoes, I want to get another pair." That would be ἄλλον.

The word that John uses here for the Holy Spirit is ἄλλον. So, the Holy Spirit is the one who comes alongside us like Jesus comes alongside us. Who helps us as Jesus helps us. The Holy Spirit helps us carry on the ministry of Jesus because the Spirit is like Jesus.

We know that Jesus has the same nature as the Father, we see that in what he says and does—so it makes sense then that the Holy Spirit also shares that nature. The Holy Spirit is God, drawing alongside us, as a comforter, helper, encourager and as the one who empowers. We need to live in his power, God who is with us every day, in every place we step, as the gift given by Jesus himself. The Spirit is the ever-present reminder that God is the God who gives himself. The Spirit is God giving himself to be with us, the fulfilment of the promise Jesus made at the great commission—"I am with you always."

So, if we want to be like Jesus, to have character shaped like Jesus, then we need to rely on the Holy Spirit. What does Jesus shaped, Spirit empowered, character look like?

THE FRUIT OF THE SPIRIT

When Jesus appears on the public scene in Luke 3, he comes to his cousin John to be baptized:

---

23. John 14:16–17a.

> "When all the people were being baptized, Jesus was baptized too. And as he was praying, heaven was opened and the *Holy Spirit descended on him* in bodily form like a dove. And a voice came from heaven: 'You are my Son, whom I love; with you I am well pleased.'"[24]

For Jesus, his identity as the Son of his Father is confirmed by the Holy Spirit resting on him, and Luke then records that Jesus goes out into the wilderness *"full of the Holy Spirit."*[25]

Having come through that time of testing, remaining faithful to the Father despite the great temptation where the first and every subsequent human being had fallen short, he returns to Galilee *"in the power of the Spirit."*[26] He stands at the local synagogue in the town he grew up in and reads the words from the prophet Isaiah which began:

> "The Spirit of the Lord is on me, because he has anointed me . . ."[27]

His baptism, wilderness temptation, and ministry are steeped in the power of the Holy Spirit. His very identity is confirmed by the anointing of the Holy Spirit, and the subsequent manifesto of his Kingdom; to proclaim good news to the poor, bind up the broken-hearted, proclaim freedom for the captives, release from darkness for the prisoners and to proclaim the year of the Lord's favor, flows from the indwelling and anointing of the Holy Spirit.

The ministry of Jesus is the ministry of the Holy Spirit, and all that Jesus did, and all of who he was, was saturated with the Spirit.

So, we who are called to carry on his ministry in the Spirit's power, who are called to bear the Maker's mark, having character shaped like Jesus, need to live anointed and indwelt by the Holy Spirit.

What is the result of this?

We turn to Paul's letter to the Galatians:

> "But the fruit of the Spirit is love, joy, peace, patience, kindness, goodness, faithfulness, gentleness and self-control. Against such things there is no law."[28]

---

24. Luke 3:21–22.
25. Luke 4:1a.
26. Luke 4:14a.
27. Luke 4:18a, Isaiah 61:1a.
28. Gal 5:22–23.

The Mark

Here we see the Maker's mark, which so clearly marked the life of Jesus and is to be our mark as we seek to live like him. This is God given, Jesus shaped, Spirit saturated character at its most beautiful and impacting. When we live in the power of the Holy Spirit as Jesus did, our character is shaped and changed to be more like his. Our lives start to bear fruit, like a tree that has the right nourishment and soil and conditions to grow. We grow in character. And what does that look like? Love, joy, peace, patience, kindness, goodness, faithfulness, gentleness and self-control. Which one of us doesn't need more of this fruit in our lives? I know I do.

But this is far more than simply a list of virtues that we need to try and live by. A list of dos to weigh against the don'ts and if the balance is right, you are doing well. No, this is about identity.

Who we are, as we began this book with, is something we need to constantly rediscover in the light of Jesus.

Several years ago, on my birthday I took a DNA test to explore my ethnicity. I knew that we had some Viking heritage in my family, and I was curious as to what the test would show. So, I ordered the kit online, provided the saliva sample that it requested, sent it off and waited for the results. Some of what came back I had expected, but some of it I had not. English, Northwest European, Scandinavian—yes. Middle Eastern and Central Asian—no. To be fair the latter were small percentages but there none the less, which was a surprise.

It turns out that who we are is often an unexpected mix, but that doesn't tell the whole story. That DNA result can give me the make-up of my ethnicity, but it can't really tell me anything about who I am.

For that we must go back to the beginning. I am one who bears the Maker's mark. I am good and created in his image and likeness. I am being shaped into the likeness of Jesus, little by little through the work and power of the Holy Spirit.

Whatever my ethnicity, background, past, present or future—this is who I am. It is the line that my life is being shaped on. What that looks like in reality, is the fruit of the Spirit. That is character!

And this is a partnership, the Divine/human partnership we see so perfectly on display in Jesus. If it was solely down to me to try and be more loving, joyous, peaceful, patient, kind, good, faithful, gentle and self-controlled, then I might manage ok, at least for a while. I would imagine that like most of you there are times when I can be all these things, but if this

The Maker's Mark

is solely an effort on my part there is often an absence of a deeper process taking place at the very core of my identity.

> "Therefore . . . continue to work out your salvation with fear and trembling, for it is God who works in you to will and to act in order to fulfil his good purpose."[29]

The *therefore* at the start of Philippians 2:12 links it with the section before which is about how our *attitude* should be the same as Christ Jesus, made in the image of God but who became human. The way we think and see ourselves should be shaped like Jesus.

And again, we see that partnership coming through clearly. We are to work out our salvation, realizing that it is God who works in us.

A healthy tree in a healthy environment will produce healthy fruit. The apple tree does not need to put extra effort into growing apples; that is what an apple tree does. It produces fruit.

But it needs to be in a good environment to do what it was created to do, and that environment often needs to be tended to.

In our garden there is an area where several of our plants have died. It doesn't matter what is planted there, it seems to stop thriving and wither away. Whether it is plants that we have moved from other areas of the garden, to long established trees. There is something in the soil. Horticulturalists understand that healthy soil is a dynamic environment where life can grow and flourish. Unhealthy soil damages the potential for growth. There is potential in healthy soil, and there is potential in the soil of your life and character too. It is God who does the planting, God who does the growing, God who produces the fruit through his Spirit, but we are called to take care of the soil. To make sure that the environment of our hearts and lives is dynamic and healthy. To do that there will be stones and weeds that we will need to remove from the soil to protect the growth potential. Each fruit of the Spirit we look at in turn, we will look at what these rocks and weeds are, the damage they cause and the importance of removing them. In this way we are working alongside the master gardener in producing a fruit harvest in our lives, as it was in the Lord Jesus.

In the remaining chapters we will explore this fruit together. What it looked like in the life of Jesus and what it might look like in our lives too. As Christopher Wright points out when looking at this passage in Galatians,

---

29. Phil 2:12–13.

the fruits "do not focus on what kind of performance we can achieve, but what kind of person we are."[30]

That is going to be the shape of our discussion too. Who we are. We bear fruit because we are living consistently and authentically as those who God made us to be. God is working that process in us, slowly and seasonally in our lives, and that is where we see the partnership with our creator.

Christian character is shaped in the likeness of Jesus and is the produce of the Holy Spirit. As I said earlier in this chapter, this is about transformation.

As the prophet Ezekiel writes:

> "I will give you a new heart and put a new spirit in you; I will remove from you your heart of stone and give you a heart of flesh."[31]

It is the Holy Spirit who transforms our hearts when they are hard like stone and hard to plant in, to warm, living and dynamic places that produce *love, joy, peace, patience, kindness, goodness, faithfulness, gentleness and self-control.*

As we explore these fruits together, may we see with greater clarity who Jesus is, and in seeing him may we become more like him; and in becoming more like him may this fruit be grown more and more in our lives, reaping a harvest that nourishes us and all around.

QUESTIONS FOR REFLECTION

1. What is your life shaped on?
2. "Jesus shows us what it looks like to be fully human." Does that change the way you look at yourself?
3. How do we make God in our own image?
4. What is God stripping away from your identity for your true self to be revealed?
5. How much do you rely daily on the empowering of the Holy Spirit?
6. Are there any fruits of the Spirit you long to see in your life?

---

30. Wright, *Cultivating the Fruit of the Spirit,* 22.
31. Ezek 36:26.

3

Love

As we begin to look at the fruit of the Spirit, it is important to remind ourselves that this is not merely something we do, but rather this is deeply about identity. If it was simply about *being loving,* then we could all think of friend or family members who fit that description but who do not know Jesus. If we remove the roots, then the fruit will wither and die.

The most important aspect to this first fruit of love, whatever it goes on to look like, is that it comes from somewhere:

> "Dear friends, let us love one another, for love comes from God. Everyone who loves has been born of God and knows God. Whoever does not love does not know God, because God is love. This is how God showed his love among us: he sent his one and only Son into the world that we might live through him. This is love: not that we loved God, but that he loved us and sent his Son as an atoning sacrifice for our sins. Dear friends, since God so loved us, we also ought to love one another. No one has ever seen God; but if we love one another, God lives in us, and his love is made complete in us."[1]

Love comes from God. It is God who has poured his love into our lives; it flows from him out into the cosmos, to you and me and all creation.

And in understanding that God is the origin of love, what we see is not only the direction, that love comes first from him, but also the substance. In verse 8 of the passage above we have one of the most profound statements

---

1. 1 John 4:7–12.

ever written: God is love. Perhaps this is the greatest phrase ever written in the history of the world. This is what I mean about substance. John isn't simply saying that God is "loving." That he is the supreme director of the force of love. Although that is true, the love that we see revealed in God as Father, Son and Holy Spirit is so much more than that.

He is not saying that one of God's activities is *to love* us, although this is also true.

The amazing thing about these amazing three words, what makes them so incredible is that John is saying that everything that God does is born out of love; there can't be anything he does that isn't rooted in love. It is the essence of who he is, Father, Son and Holy Spirit, existing in perfect loving relationship throughout time; love pouring out from all that God is.

Remember I mentioned in the last chapter, this is about God before it is ever about us. What John is doing here is getting us to reflect on who God is and what he is like, because as we do that then we begin to become like him. For us to think about what it means for love to grow in our lives as a fruit of the Spirit, we need to understand the origin of love.

THE IMAGE OF JESUS

It is important to begin with how Jesus bore these fruits in his life and ministry, and this is something we will do with each fruit going forward.

The challenge as we come to the fruit of love is that, as we have already discovered, everything God does flows from him as an act of love. So, what example can you choose?

Picture the scene with me. It is the night of Jesus' arrest, and he is sharing the Passover meal with his disciples. It was a meal that they had shared together before but this time it felt different. Passover was a time of looking back in celebration, but the atmosphere on this evening was one of tension thinking about what was to come.

John sets it up for us:

> "It was just before the Passover Festival. Jesus knew that the hour had come for him to leave this world and go to the Father. Having loved his own who were in the world, he showed them the full extent of his love."[2]

---

2. John 13:1.

Jesus knew that the hour of his death was approaching fast, which makes what he did next even more incredible. What did that expression of love look like?

> "Jesus . . . got up from the meal, took off his outer clothing, and wrapped a towel around his waist. After that, he poured water into a basin and began to wash his disciple' feet, drying them with the towel that was wrapped around him."[3]

There really is no way around it; what we see here as Jesus washes the disciple's feet is spectacular and sensational! Yet intimate and gentle.

As we begin to think about what love is, and the example of love in the life of Jesus there is so much here for us to get our heads around and our hearts into.

There is no puffed-up positioning here. Jesus takes on the role of the lowest slave. Back in the time of Jesus people used to wear sandals, and the streets they walked down were not just dusty, but full of animal droppings and general filth. There were no sewers, and so whatever was around ended up on your feet. So, the act of washing someone's feet as a gesture of hospitality was reserved for the lowest slave.

Think about that for a moment, that the God of all creation who is worthy of all praise, honor, glory and power takes the position of a slave. The hands that flung stars into space, cleaning between dusty, mucky toes.

It turned the order of the world on its head, where the inferior washed the feet of the superior; the disciple washed the feet of the master; the lowest person washed the feet of the king.

The King would never kneel in front of his subjects or the master in front of his disciples.

Jesus is bringing in a new way of being, a new way to love born out of a new depth of relationship we have with the Father through him. That *his* love is linked to us in a profound and new way; that he enters our lowliness; our humanity; our dustiness and dirtiness and in finding him there, we can truly find who we really are too. Jesus chains himself to our freedom. We cannot find freedom to be who we are created to be, other than through him in moments like this. Spectacular yes; sensational, of course; but intimate and gentle and full of love.

So often the disciples didn't get it, and before we sit in judgement on that I'm certain we wouldn't have got it either. How could we, how could

---

3. John 13:4–5.

anyone grasp the magnitude of a love like this? A love that casts aside position and serves the other. A love that rejects power to bless the powerless. Part of the reason the disciples didn't get it was that this was not the world they knew, and it isn't the world we know either. If you look at the world around you, on the news, on social media, or even at times within the church, don't we all want to make friends with people at the top rather than the people at the bottom?

So, Peter's protest shows us an attitude that is easy to understand. That's the way the world is structured. Like a pyramid. At the top are the rich, powerful, and intelligent; and at the bottom are the poor, the immigrants, and the social outcasts who become the slaves of our society.

And here we have Jesus, who is above everything, taking his place at the bottom.

But what the disciples don't understand is that Jesus has come to transform the way we see the world. We are no longer looking at society as a pyramid but as a body. We are no longer looking at those who are at the top and have value and worth because of their position; or those who are at the bottom who have no value or worth except to prop up the people at the top. In a body everyone has a part to play, everyone has a function, everyone has value. Everyone has a place. In the devotional book we read each morning as a family, Louis Giglio reminds us:

> "It's easy to think that some jobs are better, or even "godlier" than others. But that's not true! Every job is important."[4]

Everyone is dependent upon the other. In the world that Jesus is bringing in, there is no last place!

Peter protests, and the words of Jesus seem a little harsh to Peter, don't they?

> "Unless I wash you, you have no part with me."[5]

What is Jesus saying? Well perhaps he is saying something like this. Unless you are part of what I am doing here; unless you are prepared to love like this, to lay aside the pyramid thinking of the world as it is, then you cannot be my disciple. You cannot follow me if you are not prepared to go where I am going. You can't follow me unless you're prepared to do what I do. You

---

4. Giglio, *Indescribable*, 138–39.
5. John 13:8b.

cannot follow me unless you are prepared to wash the feet of those who the world sees as beneath you.

This is a teachable moment. Knowing this is the last time they are all going to be together before his death, Jesus could have chosen to teach them about anything. What he chooses to do is to show them what love looks like, and then to give them a new way to follow.

Jesus continues:

> "Now that I, your Lord and Teacher, have washed your feet, you also should wash one another's feet. I have set you an example that you should do as I have done for you. Very truly I tell you, no servant is greater than his master, nor is a messenger greater than the one who sent him. Now that you know these things, you will be blessed if you do them."[6]

The word that Jesus uses here is interesting. When he uses the word example, it can also be translated as "pattern." When someone in the ancient world did a piece of art or designed something, they would sometimes do a tracing, or a pattern so that others could do what they had done as well. That is the kind of word that Jesus is using here.

He has shown love in an incredible, beautiful and symbolic way; but he has shown love as a pattern with the desire that we are to do it as well.

I remember leading a men's retreat day in a previous church, and as part of that we had a moment of washing feet. Even though they knew what was coming, it was still a profound and yet uncomfortable moment, especially for the ones who were having their feet washed. There is something interesting in that isn't there? Because in this precious exchange it is not Jesus who is uncomfortable, it is the disciples. It is not the giver but the receiver. When it comes to love that is often the way too, that we are at our most uncomfortable when we receive love that we do not feel worthy of receiving. There may be some of us who feel that there is too much hurt or too much shame to receive that kind of love. When Jesus offers it to us, as John goes on later to say, lavishes it on us,[7] we protest.

There is a different dimension to the exchange between Jesus and Peter, where we can take from Jesus' words something like this.

"Unless you can receive this love that I bring you, then there is no way that you can follow me in doing what I do."

---

6. John 13:14–17.

7. 1 John 3:1.

You cannot give what you have not received, and that is why John reminds us that love comes from God. Jesus wants to take those ashes of hurt and shame carried in your heart and turn them into beauty, if you will give them to him. When we do, we are free to receive the beautiful love he has for us, and then also pour it out to those around us.

Do we have to wash people's feet? No, although there is something very powerful about doing that, and many churches will at some point in the year re-enact this moment. It is a symbolism of something greater.

In the tradition I am part of, when we share communion together, we speak of the bread and wine as the body and blood of Jesus ... but they are symbolic.

Symbols are important because they take us to a deeper meaning. They require us to look beyond what we see; to avoid the temptation to merely copy; and to explore and express something deeper.

Water in Baptism is symbolic.

Oil when we anoint a person for healing is symbolic.

Each of those things takes us deeper—beyond ritual and into relationship.

How are we to love those around us? How are we to love one another? How are we to love our communities? It comes as we become less concerned with how we look; with our own pride and position; and become in tune with following the pattern of love Jesus set out for us.

This is love that both comforts and challenges us. Serves us and calls us to serve others.

> "A new command I give you: Love one another. As I have loved you, so you must love one another. By this everyone will know that you are my disciples, if you love one another."[8]

Discipleship is a popular word now and as we have already explored; the role of a disciple is to carry on the ministry of Jesus in the power of the Holy Spirit. It is to do what Jesus does. To be like Jesus. To bear his mark: like master, like servant. When we love others as Jesus did, laying aside self-position and taking the role of a servant, we show that we bear his mark. We reflect his character.

---

8. John 13:34–35.

THE FRUIT OF LOVE

We have seen that love marked the life and ministry of Jesus, and that we are to follow in his pattern. In fact, when it comes to love Jesus highlights its central and overarching importance to every other commandment. When asked what the greatest commandment in the law was, Jesus replied:

> "'Love the Lord your God with all your heart and with all your soul and with all your mind.' This is the first and greatest commandment. And the second is like it: 'Love your neighbor as yourself.' All the Law and the Prophets hang on these two commandments."[9]

Everything else hangs on our call to love God and to love others. In fact, our love for God spills out and overflows into our love for others, and it is this love, the love for others, that I think is the primary focus of this fruit of the Spirit.

We know it is important, we know it should be a defining mark of our lives in our goal to carry on the ministry of Jesus in the power of the Holy Spirit, in being shaped more and more into his likeness; but what does this love look like? Practically, day to day?

Love is far more than a feeling or being nice to someone. We use the word love so casually in our culture. "I *love* what you're wearing." "I *love* pizza." "I *love* what you've done with the place." Because we use it so casually it can be hard to really see what it means, and therefore how we are meant to model it in our day to day lives.

We use the same word to describe very different attachments in our lives. One word, with different meanings. In the Bible there are different words for love:

- *Agape*—used to speak of God's love that he has for the world and that Christians are supposed to emulate.
- *Philia*—friendship or comradery.
- *Eros*—romantic or sexual love
- *Storge*—familial love like that of a mother for her baby or of a brother and sister

The word Agape is the most used word for love in the New Testament and is the word used in Galatians 5 for the fruit of love.

---

9. Matt 22:37–40.

When we need help in knowing what this love looks like, we also find it in a passage that you've heard most often read at a wedding, in fact at most Christian weddings that you have been to.

> "And yet I will show you the most excellent way. If I speak in the tongues of men or of angels, but do not have love, I am only a resounding gong or a clanging cymbal. If I have the gift of prophecy and can fathom all mysteries and all knowledge, and if I have a faith that can move mountains, but do not have love, I am nothing. If I give all I possess to the poor and give over my body to hardship that I may boast, but do not have love, I gain nothing.
>
> Love is patient, love is kind. It does not envy, it does not boast, it is not proud. It does not dishonor others, it is not self-seeking, it is not easily angered, it keeps no record of wrongs. Love does not delight in evil but rejoices with the truth. It always protects, always trusts, always hopes, always perseveres. Love never fails."[10]

This passage is sandwiched between teaching on the Spiritual gifts, and here Paul reminds us that we can be doing all the right things, for all the reasons, but if we don't love then we are nothing more than a noisy symbol. What matters is how we love.

As a family we are constantly realigning ourselves along those lines. My wife Bex is so good at bringing us back to that, that what matters most is how we love.

As we seek to carry on the ministry of Jesus in the power of the Holy Spirit, for many of us that ministry will take place most immediately in the context of home. Family and friends. So, this list that Paul gives us of what love looks like is helpful to us as we try to live in the likeness of Jesus.

Before we look at these aspects of love, it is important to remind ourselves that we are not simply talking about a feeling of affection. Agape love is a demonstration of commitment that is shown in how we act towards people whether we have feelings for them or not. It is a choice.

Its equivalent word in the Old Testament is *Ahava*, which has a similar meaning, choosing to love even when it's hard. It's about commitment and loyalty. When we look at the root of the word, *ahava*, it means "I give." Of course we see the greatest act of love in the giving of God's own Son.

---

10. 1 Cor 12:31b—13:8a.

Biblical love, the Love of God, the love modeled in Jesus which we are to follow the pattern of is a love we choose to give, even when it's hard. It is deep, strong, and committed, binding itself to the other.

"Love is patient, love is kind."

Love begins with patience and kindness. So easily this is where we can fall short in the way that we are with others. One of the reasons for that is that we believe that to be patient or kind is simply about behavioral modification: if I act more patiently or kindly then that's what matters. On one level that's true, but real change, lasting change comes from a change in heart, a transformation of attitude to mirror that of Jesus. Bearing his mark of love is reflecting his true character, and for Jesus that was not simply that he was more loving than anyone else, but it was born out of a deep-rooted identity and a heart that was directed towards the Father.

An important mindset in becoming more patient and kinder in the way we love is to learn to see others as Jesus sees them. To realize and understand that I am not the only one that Jesus loves, and that I am not the only one that Jesus is working on. That might seem small, but when I understand that the other person is deeply loved by Jesus, and on that same journey of transformational renewal then it will change the way that I act towards them. When my heart towards them has changed, then so will my actions.

When we are impatient and unkind, we have lost the battle in our hearts long before words leave our mouths. Patience is understanding that God has not finished with either myself or the other person, and kindness is seeing the other person through the lens of a loving heavenly Father.

I recently came across this definition of kindness:

> "Kindness is the sincere and voluntary use of one's time, talent, and resources to better the lives of others, one's own life, and the world through genuine acts of love, compassion, generosity, and service."

It is a voluntary action, and what that means is that I must choose to do it. That is easy when the other person is behaving in a way that easily draws patience and kindness from us, but what about when they aren't? That is when I must choose to be patient and kind. That is when I must remind myself of how God sees them. When I am tempted to look judgingly at the heart of others, that is when I need to look at my own heart the most.

We will go on to explore both patience and kindness in more detail later.

"It does not envy, it does not boast, it is not proud. It does not dishonor others; it is not self-seeking . . ."

Having started with what love is, Paul now reminds us of what love is not. Again, there is a call to lay aside a focus on ourselves. While envy is directed at other people or things, it's a lot closer to home. Envy is about a lack in us, that we believe (wrongly) can be filled with something *out there*. Why am I envious of my neighbor's house? Because I believe that if I had that house then my life would be better. It's not really about the other house at all, but about the lack in me; the hole in my heart that needs to be filled.

The same can be true for pride and boasting. That all comes from a sense of ego. If I want to feel important then I need to puff myself up to others, and that usually comes through comparing myself to someone who I think isn't quite as good as me.

All these things come from that attitude of self-seeking, of thinking that I am the most important thing in my life. Whether it is looking at what others have in a desire to be *better*, or pushing myself up at the expense of others, it all comes from the belief (or lack of belief!) in my own importance or simply wanting to be right.

Let's think back to the example of Jesus as he washed the feet of his disciples. Is that what we see there? No, not in the slightest. What we see there is love that lays down itself in surrender to the good and the blessing of the other. Again, it is a choice, to lay oneself down and to love the other. When we can do that, when our hearts are transformed by the Spirit to reflect Jesus in that way, then we can celebrate what others have without there being a lack in us; we can celebrate the achievements of others without having to highlight our own; then we can seek the good of others without fear of missing out.

" . . . it is not easily angered; it keeps no record of wrongs."

We live in a cancel-culture that is not only easily angered by the wrongs of others but seeks to cut them out altogether as a result. Which raises the question of whether we are actually living in a *throw-away* culture? A culture that discards others when they don't measure up.

That raises a challenge for us to live differently, and to love in the opposite spirit we see in the world.

Keeping no record of wrongs is more than simply holding our tongue. It goes beyond simply not responding when someone does something we perceive as wrong, on multiple occasions. It is being able to deal with each offence as it comes to the degree that you can lay it down. So, when the next one comes you aren't piling on top of offences that you have held onto in your heart against the other person. That may or may not be possible to raise with the person who has wronged you, but it is certainly possible to bring this to God. If someone has wronged you, then bring that hurt and pain to God and ask for the strength to forgive. That forgiveness is not about forgetting, any more than keeping no record of wrongs is about forgetting. Some wrongs can't and shouldn't be forgotten. It is about the transformation that takes place deep within us towards the other person where that wrong is not something we hold over them or stack up against them. As Gary Chapman reminds us in his book *The Five Love Languages*:

> "Love doesn't erase the past, but it makes the future different."[11]

This is a long-term thing. It is remembering that our character reflects Jesus', and that our lives not only bear his mark but are modeled and shaped on him. Being human, Jesus would have been hurt by the actions of others. He forgave them. He never kept score.

As those who follow him, we are called to do the same. When we are tempted to keep score, or to add to a pile of grievances, we can take the hurt to our Father and let him bring healing to our hearts. As Paul says to the Ephesians:

> "Be kind and compassionate to one another, forgiving each other, just as in Christ God forgave you."[12]

Love gives the benefit of the doubt. Love is choosy, it chooses what it keeps. What do you choose to call to mind when they wrong you? Do you get out the calendar in your mind and think "on the 22nd September you said or did this, and I've been holding it all that time, and now's the time it's coming out!" Or do you fill your mind with the best, the beautiful, the praiseworthy things in that person, as well as the stupid thing they just said or did. If you're going to keep a record, let it be those things, not the wrongs.

---

11. Chapman, *Five Love Languages*, 143.
12. Eph 4:32.

> "Love does not delight in evil but rejoices with the truth."

Do not go looking for the wrong in others. So much gossip is caught up in this; "did you hear what John did last week . . . " When a friend, brother, sister, or spouse makes a mistake, or slips and falls, that is never something to be pleased about. That is why tabloid newspapers and gossip columns are such best sellers. Or the feeds that come up on social media. There is nothing we love more as a society than tearing someone down rather than building them up.

Bad news, fake news, is what sells in today's world, and the reason why it sells is that we want to read it. If we didn't want to read it then it wouldn't sell.

That is what make us different as followers of Jesus. We do not focus on what is evil or wrong, but we delight in what is true.

Paul encourages us:

> "Finally, brothers and sisters, whatever is true, whatever is noble, whatever is right, whatever is pure, whatever is lovely, whatever is admirable—if anything is excellent or praiseworthy—think about such things."[13]

This is real love in action. To choose to focus on these things in a world that so often shows the opposite takes the filling and empowering of the Holy Spirit. This kind of love is honest. True love that is born of the fruit of the Spirit doesn't sweep sin under the rug. Love doesn't try to excuse bad behavior or put up with injustice. It treasures truth, celebrates good behavior, and prizes honesty. It has nothing to hide because it seeks to walk in the light of truth.

> "It always protects, always trusts, always hopes, always perseveres. Love never fails."

There is consistency here. Always. Not when I feel like it, or when the other person deserves it, or when circumstances allow it. Always! We are consistently inconsistent with the way we love. Thank God he doesn't love us like that. If we are to grow more and more into the character and nature of Jesus, then we need to pray for more consistency in the love we show.

Love always protects. The word here is like a roof over your head. That there is no danger that can come upon you because there is something solid

---

13. Phil 4:8, *Message*.

and sure above you to shield you from danger. That you are cared for and watched over. That "His banner over me is love."[14]

Love always trusts. It looks to see the good in the other. It gives the benefit of the doubt.

Love always hopes. Love is always looking for a future. In good times and in hard times, in times of joy and times of suffering. Paul says to the Romans:

> "We also glory in our sufferings because we know that suffering produces perseverance; perseverance, character; and character, hope. And hope does not put us to shame, because God's love has been poured out into our hearts through the Holy Spirit, who has been given to us."[15]

Hope does not disappoint, because God's love has been poured out into us by the Spirit. The fruit of the Spirit is love, so that love can be full of hope as our character is shaped to be more like Jesus', even through the hard times.

Love always perseveres. Love keeps on trying, keeps finding a way. It is an action not an intention.

Of course, we all have people we dislike. We all have people we would rather not associate ourselves with. This occurs as much for those within the church as those outside the church. Whether our separations are based on political, social, or theological divides, we all have people that we see as "the other." This is a part of the fallen nature of humanity. Christ, however, empowers us to move beyond this. Christ calls us to love those whom he loves, to serve those whom he serves, and to be as radical in our expressions of this love as he was. If Christians would but fully embrace the spirit-filled, Jesus focused way of agape *love*, we could, quite literally, change the world.

TENDING THE SOIL

If this is the love we see modeled to us in Jesus, which the Spirit is bearing as fruit in us little by little, then how can we help in this process.

Firstly, there are some weeds that we need to remove from the soil of our hearts to make our lives healthy ground for growth.

---

14. Song 2:4.
15. Rom 5:3–5.

Indifference.

Because we know the passage in 1 Corinthians 13 so well, we tend to forget how profound this is. Paul's words here are as life-changing today as they were in the first-century world. In an age known for its cancel-culture, the call to be patient and kind is radically transformative. Christ calls us to express love to those *outside* our circles of friendship and communion. Make no mistake, Christ's love is to be expressed to the very people we would otherwise choose to ignore. The person we sigh at the thought of serving and the people we wonder if it is possible to love in this way.

This is why we need this love to be born in us through the Holy Spirit.

Sometimes we are in danger of limiting the scope of this fruit of love and becoming indifferent to those who fall outside of our limited scope. The opposite of love isn't hate, it is indifference. It is not caring at all. It is failing to see the worth of the other.

If there is a person or group of people that you struggle to love, then we can be sure that it is to *them* that Christ's love is to be expressed. Echoing Jesus' parable of the Good Samaritan, Christians are called to express *agape* love to the very people we may be tempted to disregard or even reject. It is to those who differ from us, who may even be opposed to us that we are called to be patient with rather than dismissive. Instead of being rude, opinionated, or aggressive, Christ calls us to kindness. Pride, boastfulness, arrogance, or vanity destroys the work of Christ's love in our lives. There is no place for these things in the loving heart of the Christian.

Self-Centeredness

One of the biggest weeds that seeks to choke the life of the fruit of love is self-centeredness. Right before the list of the fruit of the Spirit, Paul lists the works of the flesh:

> "It is obvious what kind of life develops out of trying to get your own way all the time: repetitive, loveless, cheap sex; a stinking accumulation of mental and emotional garbage; frenzied and joyless grabs for happiness; trinket gods; magic-show religion; paranoid loneliness; cutthroat competition; all-consuming-yet-never-satisfied wants; a brutal temper; an impotence to love or be loved; divided homes and divided lives; small-minded and lopsided pursuits; the vicious habit of depersonalizing everyone into

The Maker's Mark

a rival; uncontrolled and uncontrollable addictions; ugly parodies of community. I could go on.

This isn't the first time I have warned you, you know. If you use your freedom this way, you will not inherit God's kingdom."[16]

Eugene Peterson catches the self-centered nature of these attitudes so well. When love is centered on self and not on others then the focus becomes solely about what I want and what I feel. We end up using other people for our own emotional and physical gratification. We see so much of this in the world around us, but the life of the Spirit and life lived in the pattern of Jesus is so much more than cheap self-satisfaction.

Paul encourages the Galatians earlier in chapter 5 to "serve one another humbly in love."[17] The word Paul uses here means taking on the position of a slave. Sound familiar? It should, because it's exactly the position we see Jesus take when he washes the disciples feel. It's laying aside your own position to love others.

In Galatians 2:20 we read:

"I have been crucified with Christ and I no longer live, but Christ lives in me. The life I now live in the body, I live by faith in the Son of God, who loved me and gave himself for me."[18]

As we come to Jesus our destiny is to become more like him. The old self has gone, and the new self in being shaped little by little into his image. To bear his character, his mark. What does that love look like? It gives to the other.

There is a battle between the flesh and the Spirit that takes place within us. We need to be honest in prayer about the state of our hearts, so that the Lord can empower us to root out and pull up the weeds of indifference and self-centeredness that would seek to limit the growth of the Spirit's fruit of love.

There is so much that could be said about love, and nothing we could say would ever be enough to give justice to the majesty and beauty of the love God has poured out to us in Jesus. How do we live in response to that love? As Isaac Watts, the writer of the great hymn "When I Survey the Wondrous Cross," confesses:

"Love so amazing, so divine, demands my soul, my life, my all."[19]

16. Gal 5: 19–21.
17. Gal 5:13b.
18. Gal 2:20.
19. Isaac Watts, "When I Survey the Wondrous Cross" (1707).

Will we hand over to the Lord all that we are so that we can be filled with his love?

The pastor and writer John Eldredge begins each day with a prayer:

> "Lord Jesus, I give my life to you today, to live your life."[20]

As we allow our lives to be filled with the life of Jesus through his Spirit, we find that he lives his life in and through us. The way we love becomes the way he loves in and through us. We are forever changed, and so is the world around us.

As the American pastor and theologian Francis Schaeffer writes:

> "Love—and the unity it attests to—is the mark Christ gave Christians to wear in the world."[21]

Love is the Maker's mark.

QUESTIONS FOR REFLECTION

1. Everything Jesus did was saturated with love. What other examples of Jesus expressing love can you think of?
2. Is there an example of someone you know showing you love in which you saw the mark of Jesus? How did that transform the situation and your life?
3. How can we take on the position of a servant in showing love to others?
4. Think of Jesus washing the feet of the disciples, even your feet. How comfortable are you with receiving this kind of love?
5. As you read the aspects of love Paul draws out in 1 Corinthians 13, which of these do you find easiest to live out?
6. Which do you struggle with?
7. Are there aspects of indifference and self-centeredness that need to be weeded out of your life?

---

20. Eldredge, *Beautiful Outlaw*, 205.
21. Schaeffer, *Mark of the Christian*, 29.

4

Joy

BAPTISMS ARE ALWAYS A cause for celebration. A person is committing to follow Jesus, to turn away from a former life and to embrace the new creation God has made them. They want to do this publicly with family and friends, often sharing testimony of how God has moved and worked in their lives. These are times of joy and celebration for the person coming for baptism, but also for the whole community who have often played a part in that person's story.

Several years ago, we had a baptism of a guy who came to faith through Alpha, who also attended an AA group meeting daily in our church. When it came to his baptism there are two things I remember vividly. The first is that the heater that normally brings the water temperature in the baptistery up to a nice warm level, had broken the night before. So, when I arrived at church that morning, the water was *very* cold, to the point that I had to check with both the people getting baptized that morning if either of them had a heart condition. Thankfully neither of them did, and even the cold water couldn't dampen the joy of the occasion.

The second thing I remember was the joy, especially from family, friends and those who came from the AA group to bring their support and celebration. Now when both those being baptized came out of the water, there was applause and cheering that erupted from those who had come to share in this moment. It was a celebration that most of the church were delighted to join in with.

However, after the service a couple were talking to one of our leadership team about how they felt this response was inappropriate. "It just wasn't solemn enough" they complained.

I remember feeling so disappointed.

Are there millions of people sitting at home and not coming to church, who long for there to be more solemnity in their lives? The opposite is true! There are millions of people at this very moment who desperately want to know what joy is, and to experience that in the day-to-day reality of their lives. Why are they sitting at home? Because they often don't see that joy in the church or in Christians.

I wonder if people came into your church, would they experience joy? When people meet you, do they catch a glimpse of that joy? Or is it so deep down in your heart that even the Chilean miners would struggle to find it? There are some Christians who talk about the joy of the Lord, but it seems like they were baptized in lemon juice.

There is no perfect definition of joy, but most of us know it when we feel it and we can spot it a mile off when it's missing. We gravitate towards its infectiousness, and we are repelled by its absence. It is a fruit of the Spirit, and in this chapter, holding all we have talked about so far, that's what we are going to explore.

THE IMAGE OF JESUS

If you were having a dinner party and you could invite five guests from history, who would you invite? Mine have always changed over the years. I think I would invite King David, Henry VIII, Jane Austen, Mother Theresa and Julius Caeser. I think that would make for an entertaining evening. It's always an interesting question to ask, and what sort of measure we use to determine who we invite. Are they interesting? What would the small talk be like? How would they engage with the other guests? Could I imagine a world where Jane Austen and Henry VIII would chat freely about the weather? Or think about Mother Theresa speaking to Julius Caeser about the importance of peace?

I always find it interesting when people pick Jesus. Give me a moment to explain before you judge me too quickly. Most of the time when we are asked this question we pick Jesus because we feel we should, because "Jesus" is the right answer to any question including who you would invite to your fantasy dinner party. Like the child when asked a question in Sunday

School about what animal is grey, furry, gathers nuts and lives in trees answers, "well it sounds an awful lot like a squirrel but I'm going to say Jesus."

In truth the Jesus that we think we know, the Jesus that sadly is so often portrayed by churches and Christians is very serious and if we are being honest, a bit intense and boring. Not really fantasy dinner material. But equally, I believe, a million miles away from the Jesus we see in scripture.

What doesn't help is that finding a clear-cut example of joy in the life of Jesus isn't straightforward either. In the previous chapter it didn't take too long to land on Jesus washing the feet of the disciples as an act of love and there were lots of other examples I could have used if not that one, but joy?

What we need when we read the Bible is to understand something of what is not explicitly being said to understand what is. That is what we call context. As Andrew Ollerton reminds us in *The Bible Course*,[1] when we take the *text* out of "*context*," what we are left with is a con.

The idea that Jesus was someone dull and boring, who didn't know how to have a good time, is one of the biggest cons going, which ripples down through the ages to some of his followers.

Jesus was a Jewish man, and as such would have been to the usual annual festivals and celebrations that were so important to his Jewish faith. Some of those festivals would involve a pilgrimage to Jerusalem and others would be celebrated locally. Shabbat was celebrated weekly, and other festivals like Passover or the festival of Tabernacles would have been celebrated annually. Likely Jesus would have celebrated all these festivals with family and friends, but only some of them are mentioned specifically by the gospel writers. John talks of Jesus celebrating the festivals of Tabernacles[2] and Dedication (Hanukkah),[3] and both Matthew and John speak about Passover[4] in Jerusalem.

These festivals were part of community life, to be celebrated with family and friends and were a time of music, food and celebrations which would have lasted several days. They were a remembering of how God had rescued his people. They were times of joy that punctuated the life of Jesus. We know that these were times to celebrate and be joyful because when they were instituted at the time of Moses, that was exactly the encouragement

1. See *Bible Course* from The Bible Society.
2. See John 7:1–14.
3. See John 10:22–24.
4. See John 2:13–25, Matt 26:17–19.

that was given; "be *joyful* at your festival."⁵ In fact, the Pharisees accused Jesus of having too much fun at festivals and parties leading Jesus to rebuke them:

> "John the Baptist came neither eating bread nor drinking wine, and you say, 'He has a demon.' The Son of Man came eating and drinking, and you say, 'Here is a glutton and a drunkard, a friend of tax collectors and sinners.'"⁶

The life of Jesus would have been one marked by periods of celebration. He would have sung, danced, and feasted.

But we also get a glimpse into the joy in the life of Jesus through his ministry.

In Luke 15 Jesus tells three parables: the lost sheep, the lost coin and the lost son.

In the parables there is something that has been lost, and in each case there is someone who goes looking for it. It has value and worth.

> "When the shepherd finds the lost sheep he *joyfully* puts it on his shoulders and goes home. Then he calls his friends and neighbors together and says, '*Rejoice* with me; I have found my lost sheep.'"⁷

When the woman who has lost her coin, which is about a day's wages, finds it, she also calls to her friends and says, "*rejoice* with me; I have found my lost coin."⁸

The third parable is one we know well. When the son returns home, he gets the unexpected welcome. The running father and the feast; both are symbolic of joy. First Century men did not usually run. To be able to run they had to hitch up their tunics, and that would have been viewed as undignified. But in the parable, we see:

> "... while he was still a long way off, his father saw him and was filled with compassion for him; he ran to his son, threw his arms around him and kissed him."⁹

---

5. Deut 16:14a, for wider context see Deut 16:13–17.
6. Luke 7:33–34.
7. Luke 15:5–6.
8. Luke 15:9b.
9. Luke 15:20.

The father is filled with compassion, but also with joy at seeing the son that was lost. So he runs. He ignores what society says he "should" do, and he runs to meet his son.

Having shown this display of joy to his son, like the shepherd and the widow, he draws others into the celebration. They have a party! "Let's have a feast and celebrate"[10] says the father.

This joy is based on love that goes far deeper than a person's circumstances. What did we think was going to happen? The father was going to wait at the house, arms folded and with a dismissive voice say to his son, "well look what the cat dragged in. You stink. What are you expecting, some kind of party? After the way you treated me and the way you've been living! You're lucky I don't throw you out of here!" I wonder if that's what we think the father in the parable is going to say. I wonder if we think that is what God the Father is going to say to us. What Jesus shows us here is that the Father greets us in joy not in judgement.

In each of the parables it is the one who searches that is the hero, and the one who searches, in finding, experiences joy. Heaven rejoices![11]

Jesus celebrated the feasts. He celebrated when his ministry brought people home to the Father. Even though Isaiah describes him as a *man of sorrows*,[12] Jesus' life was marked by joy. Donald Macleod takes it further:

> "A joyless life would have been a sinful life. Jesus experienced deep, habitual joy."[13]

Not only was Jesus a person who experienced joy, but he was a person whose very presence brings joy to others. When the angels appeared to the shepherds in the fields outside Bethlehem when Jesus was born, what was their message:

> "I bring you good news that will cause great joy for all the people."[14]

Good news that causes great joy. That's what the presence of Jesus in the world brings: great joy! His presence changes the way we look at the world around us; we have a totally new lens. No, the world is not always as God intended it to be. Yes, there is still great darkness that covers the earth

10. Luke 15:23b.
11. Luke 15:7, 10.
12. Isa 53:3.
13. Macleod, *Person of Christ*, 171.
14. Luke 2:10b.

and brings pain and suffering to many, and we as followers of Jesus are not immune from that. Jesus himself prepares his disciples for the pain they will feel at his death, but also the joy that will come with his resurrection—a joy that will last forever:

> "Truly, truly, I say to you, that you will weep and lament, but the world will rejoice; you will grieve, but your grief will be turned into joy. Whenever a woman is in labor she has pain, because her hour has come; but when she gives birth to the child, she no longer remembers the anguish because of the joy that a child has been born into the world. Therefore, you too have grief now; but I will see you again, and your heart will rejoice, and no one will take your joy away from you."[15]

In fact, the very first word Matthew records the risen Jesus as speaking is *rejoice*.[16]

We can and should see the world differently now because of the joy that Jesus brings. The world is different because of his presence. E Stanley Jones reflects:

> "The early Christians did not say in dismay, 'look what the world has come to,' but in delight, 'look what has come to the world.'"[17]

That is a challenge to us as we look at the world around us, and the world on a more global scale. Yes, there is much to be concerned about, and we have made a terrible mess as human beings when we have failed to live with the Maker's mark. However, because Jesus has come into that same world, we can know the pleasure and joy of the Father.

THE FRUIT OF JOY

I want to make something clear before we go further in this chapter. Joy is not a solely Christian emotion. Many people of all faiths and none experience joy in everyday and profound moments. The same can be said for all the fruit in their own way. That is part of the way humanity has been made in the image of God, reflecting something of his character and nature. When people experience joy it is an expression from and connection to the

---

15. John 16:20–22.

16. Matt 29:9—Although the NIV translates the Greek word χαίρετε as "greetings," in other places in the New Testament it is translated as "rejoice."

17. Stanley Jones, *Abundant Living*, 7.

joyful creator of all things, and it gives them a glimpse of the joy that can only fully be found in him.

What there is for Christians, as those who are being shaped into the character and nature of Jesus, as those who bear the Maker's mark, is an anticipation that this joy will be more consistently and fully present in our lives.

> "May the God of hope fill you with all joy and peace as you trust in him, so that you may overflow with hope by the power of the Holy Spirit."[18]

One of the challenges that we face when thinking about joy is that we often confuse it with happiness. We think that when Paul encourages us to *rejoice always*[19] that it means we must be happy all the time. As wonderful as life can be, I don't think there is one of us who could say that we are happy all the time. Importantly neither was Jesus.

Happiness

When I think about moments in my life when I have been the happiest there are two moments that stand out to me.

The first was the day that I married my wife Bex. It was a beautiful July afternoon in Devon on the South coast of England. The weather leading up to that weekend hadn't been great, but we were blessed with a warm and sunny day. We were joined by friends and family from around the world to celebrate the start of our married lives. I remember watching Bex walk down the aisle of the church and feeling so grateful to God that he had chosen such a wonderful woman to be my wife. It's a feeling that has only grown over the years and in a couple of weeks we celebrate our eighteenth wedding anniversary.

The second day was the birth of our son Leo. Also, a July event, and at the time the hottest July day on record, it was not a day to be in a hospital with windows that can only open a crack. I remember the industrial fans that they had to bring into the corridors and the wards to keep everyone as comfortable as possible. I remember the staff holding Leo up and seeing him for the first time, and the moment when the nurse passed him to me for the first time. Holding this tiny little baby in my arms,

18. Rom 15:13.
19. 1 Thess 5:16.

knowing that God had given him to us to love, care for and nurture was a beautifully happy moment. I still have those moments as he has grown, kissing him each day, doing my best to be the best father I can be to such a precious child.

Here's the thing about those two days. The sun set. The day ended. In time the memories will fade. If joy is simply about happiness, that giddy feeling when everything lines up for you then the biggest challenge that you'll face is that those moments don't last. That's not meant to sound pessimistic, because no moment can. When we experience hard and painful moments, we reassure ourselves that this too shall pass; that it won't always be like this. We are right, it won't, but the same thing that is true for the hard times is also true for the happy times.

So, joy must be more than simply being happy. I remember when I was a teenager having lunch with a friend who wasn't a believer at the local Christian café. While we were there, we had a brief conversation with one of the leaders of the church, and later as we were leaving my friend said to me, "I don't trust anyone who is that happy all the time." Now that might have been a little harsh on the part of my friend, but you get the point: happiness can't be all the time.

The Bible mentions the word joy 330 times but only mentions the word happiness 26 times. That's almost 13 times to 1 that joy appears over happiness, and I think it's important that we take that message on board. Happiness depends on what happens to you, and if everything lines up just right then you'll be happy. People spend their entire lives trying to line their ducks up right. They think that if they have the right job or the right salary or marry the right person, live in the right size house, or drive the right car—the list can go on and on—then they'll be happy. Sound familiar?

Joy is something different because joy comes from the Spirit of God. It is a fruit of the Spirit. Joy is something that is grown in you rather than something that happens to you.

Author and speaker Kay Warren puts it like this:

> "Joy is the settled assurance that God is in control of all the details of my life, the quiet confidence that ultimately everything is going to be alright, and the determined choice to praise God in every situation."[20]

Happiness is a response to something great. Joy comes from someone great.

---

20. Warren, *Choose Joy*, 27.

The Maker's Mark

Joy that comes from somewhere

Joy finds it source in God. If you look at the creation narrative in Genesis, then you catch a glimpse of the creative joy of God. You can see his joyous artistry in the variety and beauty of life he creates. When I spend time in nature, and I hear the babbling river, and see the majestic mountain, and feel the wind as it rustles through the trees, I feel a great sense of joy. God created through joy, and we feel the residue of that every time we spend time in his creation. Imagine for a moment though, that God created the world in the same way that we work? Can you imagine if joy was taken out of the act of creation? John Ortberg helps us to see what that might look like:

> "In the beginning, it was nine o'clock, so God had to go to work. He filled out a requisition to separate light from darkness. He considered making stars to beautify the night, and planets to fill the skies, but thought it sounded like too much work; and besides, thought God, 'That's not my job.' So, he decided to knock off early and call it a day. And he looked at what he had done, and he said, 'It'll have to do.'
>
> On the second day God separated the waters from the dry land. And he made all the dry land flat, plain, and functional, so that—behold —the whole earth looked like Idaho. He thought about making mountains, valleys, glaciers, jungles, and forests, but he decided it wouldn't be worth the effort. And God looked at what he had done that day and said, 'It'll have to do.'
>
> And God made a pigeon to fly in the air, and a carp to swim in the waters, and a cat to creep upon dry ground. And God thought about making millions of other species of all sizes, shapes, and colors, but he couldn't drum up any enthusiasm for any other animals— in fact, he wasn't too crazy about the cat. Besides, it was almost time for the Late Show. So, God looked at all he had done, and God said, 'It'll have to do.'
>
> And at the end of the week, God was seriously burned out. So, he breathed a big sigh of relief and said, 'Thank Me, it's Friday.'"[21]

What a difference it would make if we had a joyless creator.

Not only does God speak that joy and pleasure over creation at its source, but he speaks it over you and I even now. In fact, He sings it over us. The prophet Zephaniah writes:

"The Lord your God is with you,

---

21. Ortberg, *Life You've Always Wanted*, 62.

JOY

> the Mighty Warrior who saves.
> He will take great delight in you;
> > in his love he will no longer rebuke you,
> > but will rejoice over you with singing."[22]

When we are close to Father God we can feel the joy of his presence. When we gather to praise and worship, we get a foretaste of that joy that will be complete when we worship face to face. As David says in the Psalms, "being with You is to be full of joy."[23]

What I experience in worship is not only a sense of the presence of God, but also a profound gratitude for all he has done for me. That he has rescued me, made me a new creation, and is reshaping me into the image of Jesus.

There is a very real sense in which we have joy because we understand that now things are different, that because we have met with Jesus there is a change in our situation—that there has been a change from who we were before. The apostle Peter highlights this in his writings:

> "Once you were not a people, but now you are the people of God; once you had not received mercy, but now you have received mercy."[24]

Remember, with the fruit of the Spirit it's about transformation. It's not simply about knowing more about Jesus, but about being transformed to become more like him.

Which one of us when we come face to face with Jesus wants to stay the same? I want to be different, and that continual process of transformation, little by little, brings with it great joy. Joy that comes from God. Jesus knew *that* joy from before the creation of the world. He knows the ultimate joy of unrestricted access and relationship with the Father. You could see that in him, that he knew how to live freely and lightly. Am I being changed? Am I growing? Are you? Part of the joy that comes from the Holy Spirit is knowing that I am not the same as I was. Once I was in a place where I didn't know God and now, I am in a place where I do. That journey is not simply a line to cross but a life-long road of discipleship where I am still being shaped and molded into the person God is shaping me to be. Once we were a people who didn't experience the Love of God in our lives. Now

---

22. Zeph 3:17.
23. Ps 16:11, *New Life Version*.
24. 1 Pet 2:10.

we are a people who experience that love, and this change in our situation, as it is revealed by the Holy Spirit is a cause of great joy.

That joy can be a real strength to us in times of hardship and trial. A couple of years ago I was lecturing on a MTH course in Pastoral Theology at Waverley Abbey and the subject I was teaching on was entitled "the Theodicy of Suffering." When I arrived at reception to sign in, I gave the receptionist my name, she looked down at a list and said, "oh dear." Immediately I started to worry that I had the wrong day, or I'd arrived late. She continued by reading the lecture title in a very serious voice and then commented "well I hope you at least brought them some chocolate!" Joy is not a word that we associate with suffering.

In Nehemiah we read about the rebuilding of Jerusalem and the resettling of the city by those who were returning from exile in Babylon. There is a time of rededication, and as part of that the High Priest Ezra read from the book of the law. When the people heard this being read, they began to weep knowing that they had not been living the way that God has called them to live. Ezra then decides a change is required and encouragement and celebration is needed, so he instructs the people to have a party; to eat, drink and celebrate. How could they go from collective and profound grief to celebration? Joy! Ezra instructs them:

> "Do not grieve, for the joy of the Lord is your strength."[25]

It is this joy that comes from God, from the presence of his Spirit that can enable us, even in the middle of suffering to rejoice. Earlier in the chapter I mentioned a quote from E Stanley Jones about a new perspective on the world. Let's make that more personal. What if in the times that life can be hardest, in times of pain or trial we didn't think "look what the world has come to," but instead were encouraged to think "look who has come to my life." His presence makes a difference. His presence brings joy. After all, Paul encourages us not simply to rejoice, but to "rejoice *in the Lord* always."[26]

Joy that is *going* somewhere

Not only does joy come from somewhere, but it is going somewhere. It has a source, and it has a destination.

25. Neh 8:10b.
26. Phil 4:4.

I mentioned earlier that I love spending time in nature. There is something about the beauty and the majesty of creation that can't help but joyously communicate something of their creator. David captures this with profound beauty in Psalm 19:

> "The heavens declare the glory of God;
>   the skies proclaim the work of his hands.
> Day after day they pour forth speech;
>   night after night they reveal knowledge.
> They have no speech, they use no words;
>   no sound is heard from them.
> Yet their voice goes out into all the earth,
>   their words to the ends of the world."[27]

Even though a beautiful sunset cannot speak to me in words, it has a voice which communicates something of the joy of its creation, but also something of an anticipation of an even greater joy that is coming. When we spend time in God's creation we catch that joy, but we also share in its anticipation. There is a longing deep within us for a fuller joy, more than we have ever known. C.S. Lewis puts it this way:

> "If we find in ourselves a longing which nothing in this world can fill, then we can make the assumption we were created for another world."[28]

For Lewis, joy was "an unsatisfied desire better than any other having,"[29] which is shared by all creation. It is the great pull of our souls towards the one in whom they can find their ultimate and fullest satisfaction.

There we will joy in the song of the trees and mountains, forests and rivers; with the angels, elders and living creatures around the throne of God. Then our joy will not be a longing, or a stretching, but the most awake and alive expression that we have ever known.

We are all familiar with the word hallelujah. It has made it into our common language and has even resisted translation, like the word *Amen*. What I was really surprised to see is that this word, so common a shout of joy and song of praise with churches throughout the ages, and today, only occurs in two books of the Bible. It is mentioned less than twenty times in scripture, and only four times in the whole New Testament. In fact, in the

---

27. Ps 19:1–4.
28. Lewis, *Mere Christianity*, 120.
29. Lewis, *Surprised by Joy*, 17–18.

New Testament those four instances all occur within the same six verses; and they all come in Revelation.[30]

The last of these four hallelujahs continues "rejoice and be glad!"[31]

Praise and rejoicing find their fulfilment in heaven where all God's people are gathered.

Thinking back to Kay Warren's quote, "Joy is the settled assurance that God is in control of all the details of my life, the quiet confidence that ultimately everything is going to be alright, and the determined choice to praise God in every situation."

On that day our joy will be complete, God's reign will be fully established, everything has been made right, and we will praise God with a thousand hallelujahs with a fully alive, restored creation. No more anticipation, for all tears will have been wiped away. Or as C.S Lewis puts it:

> "Joy is the serious business of heaven."[32]

TENDING THE SOIL

I mentioned a moment ago the importance of gratitude for what God has done in shaping our joy. In light of this, one of the greatest weeds that needs to be removed from our lives is *ingratitude*.

At the root of ingratitude is a focus on our own greatness. We have seen this as a weed that threatens our previous fruit of love, and sadly it will come up again as we move through the other fruits. The danger is that as we focus more on ourselves, on what we want and our own self sufficiency then we take our eyes off Jesus. When that happens, the joy that can be found in his presence starts to fade away. We want to think of ourselves as great, wonderful and the masters of our own destiny. The truth is much more sobering. Jesus said, "apart from me you can do nothing!"[33] John puts it much more emphatically—apart from me you can do *not one thing*!

On a recent trip to the United States, we spent some time in the Rocky Mountains. It was such a beautiful place, full of mountains, rivers, forests and breath-taking vistas. Breath-taking is the correct word because we often find ourselves around two and a half miles above sea level. Where I

---

30. See Rev 19: 1,3,4,6.
31. Rev 19:7.
32. Lewis, *Letters to Malcom*, 93.
33. John 15:5.

live in Bath, we sit at a vertigo inducing, oxygen rich twenty-five meters. I struggled with the altitude. Distances I wouldn't think twice about walking at home were suddenly laborious and I sometimes struggled to breathe. There just wasn't enough air to do what I wanted to do.

When we do not have the breath of God's spirit, we cannot live for him or do the things he is wanting us to do. We need to walk in those Spirit rich places to live effectively for him. Gratitude is one of those Spirit rich places, and gratitude becomes a catalyst for joy; ingratitude is the thief of joy, it strangles it, because it ceases to root itself in all that God has done before and all that God will do in the future. It makes it all about me, and when that's the attitude of my heart I cannot bear the image of Jesus in the world.

When we forget to be grateful, all we do is focus on our troubles or the things that are going wrong in our lives.

A few years ago, I kept a gratitude journal. Is that something that you have done? Bex and I had one each, and we had them on our bedside tables so that last thing at night we could record why we were grateful. Just three things each day, one sentence for each, with a goal of bringing our minds each day to intentionally focus on gratitude.

Whether you keep a journal or make a note on a piece of paper or a device, taking time each day to record a reason for being grateful can help you to avoid a spirit of ingratitude springing up in your life. It can help to root you in the joy of the Lord, which can bring you strength even in difficult times.

The challenge to escape ingratitude is a big one, even though most of us wouldn't see ourselves as ungrateful people. A classic example comes from the Old Testament, when the people of God were wandering in the desert:

> "The Israelites said to them, 'If only we had died by the Lord's hand in Egypt! There we sat around pots of meat and ate all the food we wanted, but you have brought us out into this desert to starve this entire assembly to death.'"[34]

Let's just put that verse into context. Most of those grumbling had until very recently been slaves in Egypt. Slavery was all they had ever known. God then miraculously freed them from that bondage through a series of signs and wonders, which included parting the Red Sea so they could walk through. He led them with a pillar of cloud and then at night a pillar of fire.

---

34. Exod 16:3.

The Maker's Mark

They were alive, they were free, and they were travelling with their families under the physical protection of El Shaddai to the land he was giving to them—and *still* they grumbled! They were ungrateful. It is an easy trap to fall into. When things have been going well, it's easy to forget to be grateful for all that God has done.

Yes, they were hungry, but God had blessed their socks off! Still the temptation to grumble and be ungrateful comes in and it stole the joy right out from under them.

When things aren't going well, remember that God has rescued you. He has set you free. Don't think "what has the world come to" but think *who* has come into the world, and into your life. The God of Jacob is not only your fortress, but he walks beside you in the person of Jesus and he lives inside you in the person of his Spirit. There is so much we have cause to be joyful about. Because of his Spirit living in us we get to live like Jesus in the world, bearing his mark.

When things are going well, remember that it was God who did the rescuing, God who did the providing and God who did the blessing. Remember that moments may pass, so take time to celebrate and be joyful. Make sure that you give thanks for what God has done in your life. Write it down, remember it, and then recall it when times are tough. That's what the people of Israel did over the centuries, that Jesus and his followers were part of remembering, through the festivals. Their lives were punctuated with the joy that was germinated in gratitude. It led to celebration.

One of my favorite Psalms growing up was Psalm 107. It came to have much more meaning to me as I grew older, but even as a young person I was struck by their powerful words. The Psalmist speaks of those who wandered in the desert, unable to find a place where they could settle, who were hungry and thirsty. Maybe he has in mind the very people from Exodus 16? But the Psalm carries on:

> "Then they cried out to the Lord in their trouble,
>   and he delivered them from their distress.
> He led them by a straight way
>   to a city where they could settle.
> Let them give thanks to the Lord for his unfailing love
>   and his wonderful deeds for mankind,
> for he satisfies the thirsty
>   and fills the hungry with good things."[35]

---

35. Ps 107:6–9.

"Let them give thanks" the Psalmist says. Giving thanks in all circumstances doesn't mean that all things are good, but it reminds us of the presence of the one who is good in all circumstances. Ingratitude is a weed that needs to be removed from the ground of our hearts as we seek to partner with the Spirit in the growth of joy.

My wife Bex is a great example of finding joy in difficult seasons. There have been times in her life where she has experienced prolonged ill health, but the way she has handled these times with both joy and cheerfulness is a great example of what we have been exploring here. People have often asked her how she has managed to feel that in some of the hardest of times. Bex puts it down to God teaching her not to focus on the things that she can't do, but to notice all the things that she can still do. As she has sought to look for the positives in what is otherwise a bleak or difficult situation she has found cheerfulness, hope and joy instead of becoming downcast or despairing.

"Giving thanks is one of the most attractive things that we do. Maybe the most attractive," says Eugene Peterson.[36]

Joy is the Makers mark.

QUESTIONS FOR REFLECTION

1. If followers of Jesus are called to be joyful, why are some Christians so grumpy?
2. Are there other examples of joy in the life of Jesus that you can think of?
3. How do we often confuse happiness and joy? Can you think of examples in your own life?
4. Does your new reality in Christ bring you joy? Is this harder when you have been a Christian for a long time?
5. Does the thought of heaven bring you joy? What particular parts?
6. How can we protect ourselves daily from ingratitude?

---

36. Peterson, *Hallelujah Banquet*, 15.

5

Peace

I just want a bit of peace. Have you ever used that phrase? When it feels like you are overwhelmed or at the end of your rope, I think most of us have thought, if not said, those words. Peace is what we seek when it feels as though the world has got on top of us, and as with love and joy, we notice our need for it most when it is absent.

The time that we most come across the word peace is a place we don't consciously recall: the graveyard. Written on most gravestones over the years have been three simple letters, R.I.P: Rest in *Peace*. Is that how long we think we are going to have to wait until we get a real sense of peace?! Have you heard it from the ultra-busy person who when encouraged to rest says, "I'll rest when I'm dead!"

We live in a world that is disjointed and fractious, a world where conflict is never far from the surface and uncertainty is the watchword of current events.

Here in the UK, 14 percent of the population will experience an episode of anxiety at some point in any given week.[1] That might not seem like a large figure, but that's over nine million people who suffer with anxiety every week. Millions of homes and families are impacted every week by an illness that is slowly but surely grabbing hold of our lives. We will explore anxiety a little more towards the end of the chapter, but what this highlights is that there has never been a greater need for peace in our lives and communities.

---

1. See "Mental Health Facts and Statistics."

THE IMAGE OF JESUS

Isaiah prophetically describes Jesus as the "Prince of Peace,"[2] so who better to look at as an example as we seek to live as those who bear the makers mark of peace.

On that trip to the Rocky Mountains of Colorado, we went into the National Park and planned to take an early morning walk to Bear Lake. It meant an early start, settling off from our hotel at around 3:30am to drive to the car park at the start of the trail meaning that we arrived in total darkness. As we were some way from the nearest town of Estes Park there was no artificial light, and so we had to use torches to find where the walk was to begin. The plan was to walk by torchlight to a place overlooking the lake, where we could watch the sun come up and have some breakfast. We managed to find what we thought was a good spot (we couldn't be 100 percent sure because of the darkness) and settled down on a rock to wait for the sun to rise.

As we were sitting there in the darkness we could hear noises in the forest behind us. Noises that in the light of day wouldn't cause any anxiety at all, but that in the darkness raised the inevitable question in my mind: why did they call this *Bear* Lake? This question opened the door in my mind to a whole series of hypothetical scenarios which included how I was going to get my family safely away from the armies of bears hiding in the shadows just waiting for a continental breakfast. In the end, as you can tell, I was not eaten by bears and instead shared a beautiful sunrise breakfast with Bex and Leo, as well as several chipmunks. I am sure that I would have been spared the nervous wait for sunrise had those early pioneers named it "Chipmunk Lake." What's in a name eh?

The point of the story is this. There are times when it is natural to be afraid. There are times when, understandably, peace seems hard to grasp.

I read recently that the words "do not be afraid" occur in the Bible 365 times, one for each day of the year. As wonderfully neat as that would be, the phrase isn't mentioned that number of times specifically, although God's word does consistently address our fears. The encouragement to not be afraid is spoken in almost half the books of the Bible across both Old and New Testaments. Most of those times, the reassurance "do not be afraid" comes at times when the most natural thing to do would be to fear. Many times in scripture that's exactly where peace is needed.

2. Isa 9:6.

The Maker's Mark

When the angels appear to the shepherds in the fields of Bethlehem, they are terrified. A very natural response to a celestial being showing up unannounced at your workplace. What does the angel say to them? "Do not be afraid."[3]

As if one angel wasn't enough to terrify them, next comes a great company of heavenly hosts singing:

> "Glory to God in the highest heaven,
> and on earth *peace* to those on whom his favor rests."[4]

The coming of Jesus was an event that was to open the way of peace to all people. That because Jesus has come, we can know peace even amid darkness, uncertainty or fear, whether that's the angel-radiated fields of first century Bethlehem, the millions of homes around the country struggling with anxiety, or the chipmunk infested Lakes of Colorado.

Not only was the coming of Jesus a heralding of a new age of peace, but he modeled that peace throughout his life and ministry. As we say with joy, this wasn't because Jesus didn't know anything of anxiousness. Even a passing glance at the garden of Gethsemane would dispel that notion from our minds. But as we've just seen, peace is sometimes most evident in the places or times when we least expect to find it.

Back in 2021 I was diagnosed with two benign brain tumors, and in August the following year I had surgery to remove the larger of the two, which was about the size of an egg. I was told that the surgery wasn't difficult, but that because of the location of the tumor in relation to the main artery in the brain, it was problematic.

As the surgery approached, I was struck by a real sense of calm. So many people were praying for us as a family, from all around the world, and we could really feel the outworking of that prayer in the calmness we experienced. Of course there were times of fear. The day of the operation I had to go to the hospital alone because of Covid restrictions, and so Bex and Leo dropped me off in the car park. As I said goodbye to them I did so with a jab in the heart, would I ever see them again?

As I waited to be taken down to surgery, for the first time that fear was in the forefront of my mind. I paced up and down the pre-op room I was in, and just recited Psalm 23 over and over as I paced. Words like "The Lord is my Shepherd" . . . "he makes me lay down beside quiet waters" . . . "even

---

3. Luke 2:10.
4. Luke 2:14.

though I walk through the valley of the shadow of death, I will fear no evil for you are with me" ... "surely goodness and mercy will follow me all the days of my life." These words were a balm to my anxious heart.

Praise God the surgery was successful, and I am fully recovered, but I can attest to the painfully beautiful irony that so often peace comes in the times when we have every reason to be afraid.

In Mark 4:35–41 we read an account of Jesus calming the storm on the sea of Galilee. This was a storm that turned the hardiest of sea-faring fishermen into quivering wrecks. What was Jesus doing as all hands were on deck trying to keep the boat afloat? He was sleeping. I have great sympathy with Jesus here because I can fall asleep at the drop of a hat, but the disciples had no sympathy for their sleeping master, in fact they took it as a sign that he didn't care. Why was he asleep? Was he simply exhausted from the ministry? Probably, but it goes beyond that. Jesus had the peace to lay down and sleep because he was secure in who he was. Why fear the wind and the waves when you made them? The Creator has no need to be restless in the face of a dangerous creation. The disciples wake him up, and what happens next shatters everything they know about him to this point:

> "He got up, rebuked the wind and said to the waves, "Quiet! Be still!" Then the wind died down and it was completely calm."[5]

The wind and waves that had heard his voice at the moment of creation heard it again and they listened. Then he asks the disciples what seems like the most obvious question to answer, "why are you so afraid?"

Why was there a need to fear when you're sharing a boat with the one to whom the wind and the waves listen? His presence changes everything. It means that there can be peace even in the most terrifying of storms. Many of you will have faced terrifying storms in your lives, maybe you are going through one right now. Jesus doesn't tell us that the storm isn't scary, but he does remind us that he is with us, and that can make all the difference. As David prayed, "even though I walk through the valley of the shadow of death, I will fear no evil *for you are with me*." Jesus has peace in the storms, and because of that we can have confidence that as he walks beside us, even the wind and waves of our anxieties can be calmed and stilled.

Jesus also takes time to foster that peace in his life by taking time out. The gospels highlight on many occasions how Jesus withdrew from people, the normal activities of day-to-day life, and the demands of his ministry to

---

5. Mark 4:39.

be alone with the Father and pray. It's a major theme of the gospels, and it was this intimacy with the Father that was the source of his compassion, wisdom, power as well as the grounding of his peace. It is hard to feel peace when you are in a hurry. It is hard to feel peace when you are constantly pulled this way and that by the demands of everyday life. There need to be moments of stillness and rest, moments of solitude in life in order that we might remain close to Jesus. After all, that's what Jesus himself has called us to do:

> "Get your life from Me. Then I will live in you, and you will bear much fruit."[6]

Busyness is the enemy of intimacy. If we do not take time to get our life from Jesus, to be found in him, then how do we hope to bear the fruit of his Spirit? If we are chasing the wind by pursuing life in every other place, our work, our possessions, our finances, our health, our achievements or status, then how can we hope to understand what true peace is? We are relentlessly filling our time because of a fear of missing out. There are so many amazing things to do, places to go, and activities to take part in, which leave us with very little downtime.

Peace cannot come from all the things that the world deems as important. Many of you may already have figured that out, and perhaps some at great cost. Again, Jesus tells his disciples:

> "Peace I leave with you; my peace I give you. I do not give to you as the world gives. Do not let your hearts be troubled and do not be afraid."[7]

Are you still chasing after the peace the world gives? Do you long for a deeper peace, a far more fulfilling peace? A peace which soothes the troubled soul and brings rest to the fearful heart, because it can only come from one place. In fact, Jesus models to us a pattern of peaceful rest to follow as John Mark Comer reminds us:

> "Jesus' life template was based on a rhythm of retreat and return, like breathing in and then out."[8]

If we want to follow that pattern, to say yes to finding our peace in Jesus, then we need to say no to getting peace from the world, or rather

---

6. John 15:5, *New Life Version*.
7. John 14:27.
8. Comer, *Practicing the Way*, 57.

hundreds of no's each day. The only way to commit to finding that peace from Jesus is to seek it as he did, in the stillness and solitude of prayerful relationship. Then we can take it with us into the world, into life, into ministry.

If we are seeking to live as those being shaped into the image of Jesus, as those who carry on his ministry in the power of the Holy Spirit and as those who bear the fruit of peace, who better to learn from than the Prince of Peace himself.

THE FRUIT OF PEACE

One of the challenges of life today is that we tend to want to compartmentalize it. We've already explored that in chapter one, but I feel drawn to it again as we think about peace. If we have so many different areas of our lives, or so many different parts of ourselves, then how do we get to experience peace across them all? So, we end up breaking peace down to fit the little pieces of our lives, and we prioritize which areas we need the peace most in because we don't feel it's possible to totally be at peace. What does this peace that Jesus models to us look like? How can we bear the fruit of it in our lives and communities?

Shalom

The Hebrew word for peace that we are most familiar with is the word *Shalom*. The word isn't a state of mind or even an absence of conflict, at least not exclusively. It means wholeness.

Peace means wholeness.

We can see that right back in the story of Joseph in Genesis 43. At this point in the story Joseph is an important noble in the land of Egypt, and his brothers who sold him into slavery are coming to buy grain due to a famine in the land of Cannan. They have no idea about the real identity of the man they are buying the grain from. Then we read:

> "Then he asked them about their *well-being*, and said, 'Is your father *well*, the old man of whom you spoke? Is he still alive?' And they answered, 'Your servant our father is *in good health*; he is still alive.'"[9]

9. Gen 43:27–28, *New King James Version*.

In Hebrew, the word translated as "well-being," "well," and "in good health" is all one word—*Shalom*.

Peace is about your wellbeing, the whole of you. It is about living a *whole* life, which is a huge challenge to the fragmented lives that many of us live. That was the life that Jesus lived, and it is the life of the Spirit of Jesus living in us.

During the covid pandemic churches from around the world sung "The Blessing" over each other. I remember being so touched by that, and for a long time I couldn't listen to the UK version without crying. Our lives in that moment seemed more divided and fragmented than ever. We were kept from our loved ones, unable to embrace those we didn't live with and unable to gather to worship and pray. I was painfully aware as a pastor that our church building had closed for the first time in its history. It remained open during two world wars, but we were unable to meet for over a year. It was a time where peace was hard to find for many, and wholeness seemed a distant dream.

The words of the song are taken directly from scripture, where Moses tells Aaron the blessing that should be spoken over the people:

> "The Lord bless you
>   and keep you;
> the Lord make his face shine on you
>   and be gracious to you;
> the Lord turn his face toward you
>   and give you *peace*."[10]

That word peace . . . is Shalom. Wholeness.

Peace Comes from God

Shalom peace comes because of the blessing and keeping of God. It comes as we bask in the radiance of his face. It is not something the world can give, and it is not something we can manifest or conjure up for ourselves.

Paul prays for those he writes to in Thessalonica:

> "Now may the *God of peace* himself sanctify you completely; and may your whole spirit, soul, and body be preserved blameless at the coming of our Lord Jesus Christ."[11]

10. Num 6:24–26.
11. 1 Thess 5:23.

The God of peace. Peace comes from God. It is not the result of us working out solutions in a certain way, or the absence of certain troubling factors but it comes from the presence of God. As we have said earlier, it's not as though we can simply get away to find peace. We need to come to the one who is our peace.[12] He gives us the peace that we need, the peace that so many are seeking. In a time when people are struggling increasingly with mental health issues including anxiety, there are so many solutions that the world throws out to give us peace. Some of them are helpful to people, while others are not, but none of them will be able to give us the peace that can only come from the one who we celebrate as the prince of shalom, the prince of wholeness.

There are constant battles that take place within us, good and evil, light and darkness, wholeness and brokenness. There are times when we want to follow The Way, and there are times where we want to go our own way. There are times when we make space and take time to receive the peace that Jesus longs to give us, and times where it is crowded out by life. What happens though when the Spirit of God comes into our lives and makes a home there is that we become more peaceful and whole. If we want to know peace, transformative peace then it comes as the Spirit transforms us to be more like Jesus. As Paul says to the Romans:

> "The mind governed by the flesh is death, but the mind governed by the Spirit is life and *peace*."[13]

Peace Is Often Beyond Human Understanding.

I heard a story once about a preacher who had just delivered a very long and boring sermon. Have you ever sat through one of those? I know I've delivered some!

As the congregation was filing out of the church they had nothing to say to the preacher. After a while a thoughtful person walked by, someone who always had a word of encouragement to give at moments like this. They said, "Pastor today your sermon reminded me of the peace and love of God." The Pastor was absolutely thrilled with this comment and replied, "no one has ever said that to me before, thank you so much. Can you tell me why you thought that?"

---

12. Eph 2:14.
13. Rom 8:6.

The encourager replied, "well it reminded me of the love of God because it endured forever, and the peace of God because it was beyond all understanding!"

Paul encourages us:

> "Do not be anxious about anything, but in every situation, by prayer and petition, with thanksgiving, present your requests to God. And the peace of God, which transcends all understanding, will guard your hearts and your minds in Christ Jesus."[14]

We often think that the measure of wisdom is knowledge. It's how much we know. The same can be said for maturity. Often though it's the acknowledgment of our limitations that shows true wisdom and maturity. So, we can struggle at times with the concept of peace that is beyond our understanding because we wonder "how am I to nurture this peace in my life and encourage it to grow if I don't understand it?"

Yes, we might be called to work in partnership with Spirit of God is seeing this fruit grow in our lives, but if this peace comes from God and is born through the Spirit then we don't get to determine what that peace looks like or even where we find it. We want to know, but we are called to trust.

As we look at scripture, when do we ever see God calling us to understand him?

Paul quotes Isaiah in Romans 11:34, asking the question:

> "Who has known the mind of the Lord? Or who has been his counsellor?"[15]

God doesn't call us to understand but, in the Psalms, he calls us to:
"Be still, and know that I am God."[16]
Another way we can translate that verse is:
"Let go, and know that I am God."
He calls us to know him, to be still, let go and know his peace; but this peace is beyond our understanding because it is *his* peace. We very often recognize it as the peace of God because we find it in circumstances in our lives where we cannot imagine peace to come.

---

14. Phil 4:6–7.
15. Rom 11:34 & Isaiah 40:13.
16. Ps 46:10.

Peace can be experienced fully

> "I will heal my people and will let them enjoy abundant peace and security."[17]

Do we have a theology of scarcity or one of abundance? What do we believe about the peace that God brings in Jesus? If it is about wholeness, then it can't be about scarcity. It is full and abundant peace.

God wants us to experience his peace in abundance. It's not substandard. It is wide reaching.

One of the most beautiful passages in scripture can be found in Colossians 1. I love it in the Message:

> "All the broken and dislocated pieces of the universe—people and things, animals and atoms—get properly fixed and fit together in vibrant harmonies, all because of his death, his blood that poured down from the cross."[18]

Or as the NIV puts it at the end of that verse: "by making peace through his blood, shed on the cross."

The peace of God is so far reaching that it draws in all creation to wholeness. The chaotic fracture of sin in the world that God made is put right through peace that was won on the cross. It is full and abundant.

In Christ we see that God is not a God of half measures but a God of abundance. A God who wants us to draw close to him and experience the fullness of his peace.

There is a great verse in John 1:14 that says:

> "The Word became flesh and made his dwelling among us. We have seen his glory, the glory of the one and only Son, who came from the Father, full of grace and truth."

We have seen his Glory. The incarnation is not a theological or academic fascination, but an experience of God. It is the means through which we come to experience him. In the same way as we look at the peace of God it is not a theological or academic fascination; it is given so that we might experience him to the full.

---

17. Jer 33:6.
18. Col 1:20, *Message*.

The Maker's Mark

Peace requires the surrendering of our will

> "Let the peace of Christ rule in your hearts, since as members of one body you were called to peace. And be thankful."[19]

What does this phrase *rule in your hearts* mean?

The Greek word for *rule* is βραβευέτω, and it was a word that was most used when talking about the Olympic and other games. It's the word that refers to the director, or arbiter of the public games. An umpire. It was the role of this person to preside over the games, to preserve order, and to distribute the prizes to the winners. So, when we look at this word within the context of peace as a fruit of the Spirit and what it looks like, the meaning here is a strong one. The peace which God gives to us is like the governors at the games. It is to preside over and govern our minds; to preserve everything in its place; and to save it from all that would seek to harm it. And when we think of it like that it is a strong and beautiful thought.

We can easily find that passion and excitement can take over and rule our thoughts and our actions. Passion and excitement aren't bad. We see them in Jesus, but they shouldn't rule over us. They shouldn't be the final arbiter of our lives. We need to allow the Spirit and peace of God to keep our minds and hearts in order. It is about surrender and that is something we find hard to do.

Think about those early disciples. They followed Jesus every day for years. They walked and talked with him, they ate with him, and they lived with him. They saw the many miracles and they heard his teaching. The closer they got to Jesus the more they recognized their need for him. Sometimes our lives can show the opposite. The closer we get to Jesus, the more like him we become, the more we feel we don't need him; that we are progressing just fine.

The truth is that we cannot live for Jesus without the surrendering of ourselves. We cannot experience full and lasting peace without the surrendering of our wills. We need to give up the right to rule so that God's peace may rule in our hearts.

The fruit of peace is so much more than we can put into words. When we experience it we find a truer and fuller sense of life. That we can know it even in the middle of troubles gives us an indication that it is so much more than simply "good attitude." There is no substitute for it.

---

19. Col 3:15.

Think about your inner world for a moment, your heart and mind. Do you need more of the fruit of peace? God's shalom wholeness? What would it look like for this peace to bear fruit in your actions, thoughts and relationships? What impact would it have on your own personal inner world, family life, or your work? If peace is about living whole, then my prayer for all of us is that we might know it in ever increasing measure, flowing fully and freely from the cross of Jesus.

TENDING THE SOIL

Pastor and writer Erwin Raphael McManus reminds us:

> "The path of peace comes only when we're willing to walk into our own darkness and face our own shadows. We must face the very things that steal our peace from us . . ."[20]

Think back to the garden of Eden for a moment, and what happened on that fateful day when the peace of creation was shattered by sin. What were the consequences? Anxiety and fear, and conflict. Adam and Eve knew that they had sinned and so they hid. When God asks where they were Adam replied:

> "I heard you in the garden, and I was afraid."[21]

Suddenly the peace of God's presence was replaced by fear and it all unraveled from there. They blame each other, they blame creation, they even blame God. Conflict enters the world.

To this day, some of the biggest weeds that seek to strangle the fruit of peace in our lives are fear and conflict.

Fear and Anxiety

What are you anxious about? If we are honest most of us are anxious or worried about something. Whether it's something big, a health or financial concern, worry about a loved one; or a smaller one like packing for a holiday or making sure everything is ready for visitors.

It might be something easily identifiable. My mother-in-law was born in New Zealand and most of her family still live there. Some family live

20. McManus, *Way of the Warrior*, 10.
21. Gen 3:10.

down in Christchurch on the South Island and on 22nd February 2011 it was hit by a devasting earthquake that killed 185 people, making it New Zealand fifth deadliest disaster. When you live in an earthquake zone, or in other places that might be an area prone to hurricanes or volcanic activity, there is an element of anxiety that goes with a normal life.

It might be less easy to identify. A few years ago, when I was lecturing, that "Theodicy of Suffering" lecture, I had a strange experience on the way home.

As I got in the car to drive off, I couldn't catch my breath properly. My heart rate went up. I found it hard to calm down, and I had to pull the car over to try and control my breathing. This lasted for a good half an hour, and I wondered whether I was having a heart attack. I later learned that what I had experienced for the first time was a panic attack. It was scary and what was most scary was that I hadn't seen it coming. It had been a good day, and I wasn't worried or anxious about anything. However, I had been dealing with a very difficult and personal subject for the afternoon, and it had clearly had a more profound impact on me than I had thought. It's something that I have only experienced twice, but there may be those of you reading this for whom these types of episodes are far more regular or worse.

We should never be hesitant as Christians to get medical support. We wouldn't think twice about it if we had a thirty-minute period when our legs stopped working properly, or we lost vision in an eye. If we experience a mental issue like anxiety or panic attacks, then we somehow feel we must battle it out because there is still such a stigma around getting support for mental health. If that's something you are worried about then please go and speak to someone.

Sometimes the fear of something is natural and something God has blessed our minds and bodies with for protection. For example, I am afraid of wasps. I've been stung a couple of times and that doesn't help, it really hurts. That fear is an attempt by my mind to protect me from being stung. However, even a natural fear can be taken to unnatural levels. I remember as a child watching a TV show called 999 Lifesavers, and one week they told a story about a man who was up in his loft with his dog, and his dogs tail hit a wasp's nest, breaking it open and filling the whole loft with hundreds of wasps. I'm not too keen on going up in the loft either!

That's the challenge. It's going to an extreme. I have been stung a couple of times and yet my fear is that when I go up in the loft, I'm going to get stung hundreds of times. I have no basis for that fear and yet there have been times when as a child I would run away screaming from picnics or refuse to eat outside altogether because of this fear.

Whatever kind of fear or anxiety we experience, whether it is natural or unnatural, the reality is that we don't often get to control when it comes along. However, we can control what we do with that anxious thought or fear.

The first challenge is identifying those fears or anxieties because for many of us they aren't simple to pinpoint. We're all a little bit like scientists in that we care constantly making predictions. If this is true, then this is what will follow. Have you ever gone into a meeting with a difficult person? You know they are difficult, so you predict that it's going to be a horrible meeting, and all your energy becomes anxious as you predict all the horrible things they are going to say. You then rehearse how you are going to respond, producing all those good come-back lines and tying your stomach up in knots before you have even sat in the room with them. That's just a predicted response to something we think is coming. In her book about overcoming low self-esteem Melanie Fennel says this:

> "In fact many of our predictions are so well rehearsed and so automatic that we don't even notice them or put them into words—we just act as if they were true."[22]

When we start to feel that anxiousness and fear, we need to do something with it. Take it to the Lord. That's what Jesus does in the garden of Gethsemane. He feels afraid, he feels anxious about what is to come, so his response is to fall on his knees before the Father and ask for help. It's not to tough it out. It isn't to pull himself together. It is to seek support from the only one in that moment who could provide him with peace.

We have already seen how the peace of God is beyond our understanding and how it can be a guard over our hearts and minds. The verse before that in Philippians 4 says this:

> "Be anxious for nothing, but in everything by prayer and supplication, with thanksgiving, let your requests be made known to God."[23]

Take your requests, take your anxiousness and fear to God—so that he can exchange that for his peace. Notice here that Paul says, "*be anxious*

22. Fennell, *Overcoming Low Self-Esteem*, 102.
23. Phil 4:6.

for nothing," he doesn't say "don't *feel* anxious." It might seem like a subtle switch, but it's got big implications. Our feelings can come and go, sometimes unwelcomed and unannounced. We don't always know when we are going to feel anxious, but we can decide if we are going to *be* anxious. In other words, whether we decide to hang onto those emotions and allow them to set the direction for our lives and behaviors. Taking those emotions and feelings to God, as Jesus did, as Paul encourages us to do is the first step in receiving the peace that can then guard our hearts and minds.

In that sense our thoughts can feel a little bit like a battlefield, but remember, the battle belongs to the Lord! Even though for many those feelings of fear and anxiety don't feel like weeds at all but like great big strongholds in our lives, we have the power through the Spirit of God to see victory in those areas too. Listen to Paul in his second letter to the Corinthians:

> "For though we live in the world, we do not wage war as the world does. The weapons we fight with are not the weapons of the world. On the contrary, they have divine power to demolish strongholds. We demolish arguments and every pretension that sets itself up against the knowledge of God, and we take captive every thought to make it obedient to Christ."[24]

The peace of God can not only be a guard for our hearts and minds but a mighty power to demolish the strongholds of fear and anxiety in our lives too.

Paul encourages the Corinthians to take every thought captive. This is because the way we think has great power in our hearts. Our lives are always moving in the direction of our strongest thoughts. Its wisdom that Solomon himself knew:

"For as he thinks in his heart, so *is* he."[25]

How do we take every thought captive? Firstly, by taking it to God, and secondly by choosing to think about different things. Philippians 4 continues:

> "Whatever is true, whatever is noble, whatever is right, whatever is pure, whatever is lovely, whatever is admirable—if anything is excellent or praiseworthy—think about such things."[26]

---

24. 2 Cor 10:3–5.
25. Prov 23:7, *New King James Version*.
26. Phil 4:8.

That isn't always easy, and that is where we come back to this concept of transformation instead of information. If we are to become more like Jesus and bear his fruit of peace in our lives, then we are going to need transformation. Romans puts it like this:

> "Do not conform to the pattern of this world, but be *transformed* by the renewing of your mind."[27]

As we keep bringing our fears and anxiety before God, let's ask him to change and transform our thinking so that the strong thoughts in our minds become more about the good things he has for us.

The second weed that threatens our peace is *conflict*.

There are very few things that steal our peace as consistently as conflict. Whether it is something relatively minor, like a person in the library making too much noise, ranging to a difficult person at work or an angry driver on the road, all the way up to serious clashes or disagreements with family members or others. Conflict can come from anywhere and at any time unexpectedly.

So how do we ensure that it doesn't rob us of peace?

While we can acknowledge that conflict is a part of life, and that sometimes peace can only be found when we have moved through a conflict, it is never the ideal. As followers of Jesus who are being shaped in his image, peace is something we are called to model in our relationships:

> "For God is not a God of disorder but of peace—as in all the congregations of the Lord's people."[28]

How do I reflect something of the image of God when I come to conflict? It comes as there is a desire in me to live in peace and not stay in a place of disorder. Where my relationships are disordered and chaotic then not only are they often lacking peace, but I am not reflecting the relational heart of God—the God of peace.

I am also called to live at peace with others. Paul says:

> "If it is possible, as far as it depends on you, live at *peace* with everyone."[29]

27. Rom 12:2a.
28. 1 Cor 14:33.
29. Rom 12:18.

I both love and am challenged by how wide ranging this is. Live at peace with *everyone*. That feels like an impossible task, and Paul acknowledges that with what comes before that call to live at peace with everyone. Firstly, *if* it is possible. Secondly, as far as it depends on *you*.

It is not always possible to live at peace with people. There are some people who just do not want to be at peace. Or it might be that there has been too much damage done and the relationship is beyond repair, and we move into a space of asking God to help us to forgive. Peace in those spaces is not always possible.

It might also be that you do everything that you can do; you reach out, you try to understand, you make changes, you overcome obstacles, but the other person just doesn't want to move to the same space you do. We had that painfully with friends a few years back. There was an issue that had come up and we could tell by the way they were behaving that it was affecting the relationship. So, we invited them round to talk about it, and after a long time small talking we realized that they weren't going to bring it up. They would have happily gone home without it being mentioned. For us though we needed to move through that for peace to be restored. In the end though, if only one party is willing to participate in that then peace is hard to arrive at. You should absolutely do everything that you can do to make peace possible, but there are times when it isn't, simply because the other person isn't willing to work for it.

Those things being said, this is about the direction of our hearts. What kind of people are we called to be. Are we content to sit in the disorder of fractured relationships or are we committed to peace-making, after all Jesus said that it was the peacemakers who would be blessed for they will be called children of God.[30]

We talk about peace-making, but we often forget the second part of the beatitude. The peacemakers are blessed because they will be called children of God. Jesus is not simply referring to mediators or negotiators, but about those who carry in themselves a fulness of peace which is only accessible through sonship with God. Remember *shalom* peace. This is about wholeness that spills out from us into the world around. Why are we peacemakers? Because the Father is a peacemaker and it is the role of children to do what their Father does. Jesus shows us that heart in John 5:

---

30. Matt 5:9.

"Very truly I tell you, the Son can do nothing by himself; he can do only what he sees his Father doing, because whatever the Father does the Son also does."[31]

Why should living at peace with others be important to me? Because it is important to the Father, and because it is the Father's heart and work to bring peace and wholeness.

The fruit of the Spirit is peace. It is something we long for in our lives and in the world. We see it modeled to us in Jesus, and we can experience it fully and freely through the Spirit of God. As we continue the journey of transformation as disciples of Jesus, our characters need to increasingly bear the mark of peace. After all . . .

Peace is the Makers mark.

QUESTIONS FOR REFLECTION

1. Where are the areas of your life where you find it hard to find peace?
2. What are the ways the world gives peace? Have they been methods that have worked for you in the past?
3. How does Jesus give peace?
4. How does it make you feel to think of peace as "wholeness?" Do you think in the past you have settled for a lesser form or peace?
5. Can you think of a time when the peace of God has been present in your life, even though you haven't been able to understand how?
6. How can fear and anxiety rob us of peace?
7. Are there areas of conflict in your life where you need to experience the peace of God? How can you be a peacemaker there?
8. How will your life improve with the application and understanding of how God created us to live in peace?

---

31. John 5:19.

6

Patience

IF YOU ARE ANYTHING like me then this is the chapter you need, because if there is one thing most of us struggle with on a near daily basis then it is patience. There have been more times than I care to remember when I have been rushing out the door in the morning, needing to drop my son off at school on the way to work as the sands of patience slowly slip away through the hourglass of my life. We go five minutes past the time when we planned to leave, and I can feel myself getting agitated. I have places to go, people to see, come on let's go. I'm not as kind in how I speak as I would like to be. Everyone's stress levels are up, and all over five little minutes which when I get to work make no real difference to my day. I inevitably find myself feeling guilty for my attitude and the way I spoke.

Sound familiar?

The old saying goes "patience is a virtue"; well, it certainly is a hard one to master. If the fruit of the Spirit is the character mark of being shaped like Jesus, then it is in this area that I know I fall short the most. It is in this part of my life that I know there needs to be more transformation. It's a good job that we follow a God who is in that exact line of work, so if you feel as I do then be encouraged, he hasn't finished with us yet.

THE IMAGE OF JESUS

Jesus seems to be to have been a person of deep patience. Even before we look at some examples in the gospels let's think about the bigger picture for a moment.

God becomes human, taking on all the limitations that comes with our frail humanity, but also living bang smack in the middle of people far frailer and more limited than him. He chose followers who from day one consistently failed to get it, despite all of himself that he poured into them. He had enemies who were out to get him, constantly trying to trip him up and catch him out. To cap it all off his mission and ministry was the greatest one to have even been embarked upon and even when it was successful, people would never really be able to grasp just how much he had done for them.

It seems to me that to hold all that, you've got to be a patient person.

At the beginning of John 7 we see Jesus' brothers encouraging him to go to the festival of tabernacles in Jerusalem. The reason they are doing this is because they believe that Jerusalem is where you go to get recognized. If you want to be somebody and get a big following, then the big city is where you go to do that.

Jesus response to them is really telling:

> "Therefore Jesus told them, "My time is not yet here; for you any time will do."[1]

There are several times in the gospels that Jesus uses the phrase, as well as times when he heals a person only to ask them not to tell anyone. It seems that Jesus understood, despite the importance of what the Father had asked him to do, that there was no need to rush; there was a right time to reveal who he was to the people, and that he was content to wait for that time.

What Jesus shows us here is an important distinction between God's will and God's timing. Was it God's will that Jesus should receive glory and honor? Yes, we see that in Philippians chapter 2 were we read:

> "Therefore God exalted him to the highest place
>   and gave him the name that is above every name,
> that at the name of Jesus every knee should bow,
>   in heaven and on earth and under the earth,
> and every tongue acknowledge that Jesus Christ is Lord,

---

1. John 7:6.

The Maker's Mark

to the glory of God the Father."[2]

Was this God's timing? No.

That is often what we struggle with. Do we often think and pray, "is this the right thing? Should I do this job or go to this place?" And the answer to this question within God's will might be yes. And when we hear that answer we run ahead like a bull at a gate without waiting to see if the Lord has opened the gate or not. There is always the second question: "is it in *your* timing?" Jesus was able to be patient because he understood both the will of the Father and his timing. After all we read that Jesus came into the world "when the time was right."[3]

Jesus was also patient with his followers. As I've already mentioned these were the people that Jesus invested most heavily in during his ministry. He called them, taught them, lived with them and gave them a front row seat to most of what he did. He took time to explain to them the deeper meaning of his actions and gave them opportunities to put these things into practice. Constantly though, they failed to understand. Before we feel too sorry for them and too pleased with ourselves, do we? Do we really understand the things of Jesus? Or do we, like those early followers, get it wrong more often than we would like?

Jesus was patient with Peter after he had denied him three times.[4] Even though Peter had told Jesus that he would rather die than turn his back on him, when the time came he denied that he even knew him. Yet when Jesus rose from the dead we see the beautiful grace-filled recommissioning of Peter beside very lake where he originally called to him "follow me."

Jesus was patient with James and John when they argued about who was going to sit at his right hand.[5] Even though Jesus had been talking about a different kingdom, one where the first shall be last and the last shall be first, James and John were still seeking places of position. Rather than tearing a strip off them, Jesus patiently explains that even though he is Lord, the son of man came not be served but to serve.

Jesus was patient with Thomas when he doubted.[6] When he said he needed proof; Jesus gave him what he needed.

---

2. Phil 2:9–11.
3. See Gal 4:4—"when the time was right God sent his son."
4. See John 21:15–19.
5. See Mark 10:35–45.
6. See John 20:24–29.

Jesus was patient with Philip when he asks, "show us the Father."[7]

Jesus was patient with Peter, James and John when they fall asleep in the garden of Gethsemane.[8] At his time of greatest need, when he had taken those closest three friends with him for comfort and strength, they let him down. Still, he kept faith in them.

Repeatedly we see Jesus model patience. Yes there were times when he was frustrated, how could there not be, but through it all he modeled the same love that loyally stood by those he loved even in the face of their inadequacy.

This patience continues to his followers even after his resurrection and ascension. Paul speaks clearly of it to Timothy:

> "I was shown mercy so that in me, the worst of sinners, Christ Jesus might display his *immense patience* as an example for those who would believe in him and receive eternal life."[9]

When we think back over the times that Jesus must have shown patience to the disciples then Paul has it 100 percent right; Jesus was a person of immense patience.

Of all the times when the patience of Jesus comes across most clearly it is at the cross, where he is being executed in the most excruciating way. That's where that word comes from, excruciating means *from the cross*. It was so terrible that all the other words for pain that we had wouldn't do, so we had to make up a new one to convey just how bad it was. Jesus had been flogged to within an inch of his life. The whip used to lash him would have been made of several pieces of leather with pieces of metal near the end. It was usually carried out by two soldiers; one stood either side of the victim. These blows at full force across the back, shoulders and legs would have cut into tissue, muscle and bone, rupturing small vessels, veins and arteries. Victims of Roman flogging rarely survived.

He had a crown of thorns pressed into his scalp and temple and then was hit with sticks around the head.

Then Jesus had to carry a heavy wooden cross beam through the city, which would have weighed thirty to forty pounds and was broadly tied to his arms across the shoulders which would have been so brutally whipped. We know from the gospel accounts that after the beating he received this

---

7. See John 14:8–9.
8. See Matt 26:36–46.
9. 1 Tim 1:16.

The Maker's Mark

was too much for Jesus and he fell three times, eventually the cross had to be given to a stranger in the crowd to carry for him.

Mark states simply "and they crucified him."[10] Which fails to convey the true horror of this act to those who have mercifully never seen a crucifixion.

Jesus would have been pushed back onto the cross beam where a legionary would have hammered a large square iron bolt between the bones in the wrists. The cross beam is then lifted into place. His left foot would have pressed flat against his right foot, and with both feet flat, toes down, a nail was driven through the arch of both.

His weight pulling down would have caused unimaginable pain in his arms and wrists as the nails rubbed on the median nerves. To avoid this pain, he would have pushed up but then would have experienced the same pain in his feet. As his muscles fatigued painful cramps take hold deep into the muscles.

Because of these cramps Jesus would have found it hard to push himself up to breath out. He could breathe in but not exhale. Every breath out to avoid suffocation would have been agony. Hours of limitless pain, twisting joint-rendering cramps and breathlessness.

Then the sack around the heart begins to fill with fluid causing a crushing pain as the heart is compressed.

With the heart barely able to pump blood to his tortured body, and his lungs making a frantic attempt to gasp in small gulps of air, Jesus' body is failing. He can feel the chill of death creeping through his tissue, and he commits his Spirit into the hands of his Father.[11]

Why do I share this with you? Because in the middle of all that, somehow, miraculously Jesus prays "Father forgive them, they don't know what they are doing."[12]

I've been known to lose my temper when I stub my toe. When framed with the full horror of what he was experiencing, these words of Jesus are astounding.

There is also the patience he shows to the rebels on the cross. When one is shouting insults at him he doesn't retaliate, and when the other asks

---

10. Mark 15:24.

11. Information taken from Longman and Garland, *Bible Expositors Commentary*, 775–80.

12. Luke 23:34.

him to remember him, he doesn't say "I've got a lot going on myself here"; he reaches out in compassion and mercy. Even then. Even there.

Perhaps when I struggle with patience I need to remind myself of this. We all do. That's the savior we follow. That's the one whose image we are being made into.

THE FRUIT OF PATIENCE

What does it mean?

The word that Paul uses for Patience in Galatians 5 is *Makrothumia*, which comes from the words *makros* ("long") and *thumos* ("passion" or "temper"). This gives us a definition of patience as having a long-temper or being slow to get angry. This means that we can bear with the weaknesses, mistakes and irritations of others without losing our temper quickly.

I'm sure that you have been in a situation where there is someone, a family member, colleague, friend, who is winding you up and you can feel the tension building inside of you. You want to snap. You're losing your cool. Patience is going slowly down the drain.

We all know people who are easily irritated. Usually these people aren't shy in letting others know it, either by a steady stream of grumbling and griping accompanied by a face painted with the pain of having to suffer the fools around them; or they "blow up" in red-faced fury, shouting a torrent of harsh words intended to let everyone within hearing distance know they have "had it." So, we all know people like this, but I imagine that most of us are in between. We may not show much agitation on the outside, but inwardly we are churning with varying degrees of stress, wishing that people would "just get on with it" so we can do our thing. Does that strike a chord at all?

Ancient wisdom speaks about patience with others. Solomon writes in Proverbs:

> "Whoever is *patient* has great understanding, but one who is quick-tempered displays folly."[13]

We are called to be patient with others. Patience in the scriptures seems to have that relational dynamic. There are those in my life who need me to show patience to them, and who will receive that patience as an expression

13. Prov 14:29.

of my love for them. Remember a few chapters ago, when we looked at the attributes of love Paul lists in 1 Corinthians 13; the first attribute of love he lists is: "Love is *patient* . . . "

Gordon Fee challenges us that the Spirit's empowering isn't just that we would see miracles or have joy in our lives, but:

> " . . . also for this much-needed quality of hanging in there with those who need long and patient love and kindness."[14]

There is another word for patience in the New Testament, which is *Hupomonē*. This means *remaining under*, and it suggests the image of someone living under a burden or weight. This might be seen as more circumstantial patience. Imagine that you are going through a hard time; it might be an ongoing health issue, or facing hostility, or having to wait for something that you deeply long for. That is *Hupomonē* patience.

Let me give you an example from Jesus. When the disciples are asking Jesus how they will know when the Kingdom is going to be established, in Luke 21, Jesus talks to them about the signs that will take place before that happens. He tells them in verse 9 that even when these things have taken place, "the end will not come right away." Then he goes on to tell them:

> "But before all this, they will seize you and persecute you. They will hand you over to synagogues and put you in prison, and you will be brought before kings and governors, and all on account of my name. And so you will bear testimony to me. But make up your mind not to worry beforehand how you will defend yourselves. For I will give you words and wisdom that none of your adversaries will be able to resist or contradict. You will be betrayed even by parents, brothers and sisters, relatives and friends, and they will put some of you to death. Everyone will hate you because of me. But not a hair of your head will perish. *Stand firm*, and you will win life."[15]

The word the NIV choses to translate as "stand firm," is *Hupomon*. Bear under it. In other words, be patient and you will win life. They will be put in prison, brought before powerful and dangerous rulers, betrayed by those closest to them and even executed. Sound familiar. It should, because it is exactly what happened to Jesus. Jesus remained patient in the middle of all that suffering, in those hard times, and it is the mark of his followers that they will, in his strength, do the same.

14. Fee, *Paul, the Spirit and the People of God*, 118–19.
15. Luke 21:12–19.

Paul encourages early Christians in the same way:

"Be joyful in hope, *patient in affliction*, faithful in prayer."[16]

There are millions of Christians around the world who experience this kind of suffering each day. They know the reality of what Jesus was talking about in Luke 21 far more than we do. We are blessed with great freedom to live out our faith free from persecution or retribution. Here in the UK Christianity is the state religion, and millions go to church every Sunday without really giving a second thought to the freedom they have to do so. According to the organization Open Doors,[17] who work with and support persecuted Christians around the world, in 2023:

- 317 Million suffer very high or extreme levels of persecution.
- 4,125 Christians were detained because of their faith.
- 14,766 churches or Christian properties were attacked.
- 4,998 brothers and sisters were martyred.

The publication Christian Today estimates that 70 million people have been martyred for faith in Jesus since the days of the early church.

So, patience under hard times is infinitely more than me being annoyed that I am stuck in traffic for longer than I would want to be.

You and I may not have to go through that level of suffering or hard times for our faith, but that doesn't mean that we won't go through hard times and that we aren't required to show the fruit of patience as we experience them.

Slow to Anger

It is also important, as we say with Jesus, to remind ourselves that patience comes from God. Why was Jesus patient? Because the Father is patient, and he is the exact representation of the Father's nature.

A few chapters ago I asked what your favorite verse in the Bible was. Well now we are going to read what the Bible writers' favorite verses in the Bible were. The following passage is quoted more than any other:

---

16. Rom 12:12.
17. Statistics available at https://www.opendoors.org/en-US/persecution/countries.

> "And he passed in front of Moses, proclaiming, 'The Lord, the Lord, the compassionate and gracious God, *slow to anger*, abounding in love and faithfulness, maintaining love to thousands, and forgiving wickedness, rebellion and sin. Yet he does not leave the guilty unpunished; he punishes the children and their children for the sin of the parents to the third and fourth generation.'"[18]

This is the first time that God choses to reveal something of his character to human beings. Here God choses to share with Moses who he is, and what he is like. It comes at the moment when God is making his covenant with the people, so that they can be confident about the kind of God they are following. That he is gracious, compassionate, faithful and abounding in love are characteristics of God that we treasure and cling on to. We sing about them and hold on to them, especially when we make mistakes.

However, we struggle with a God who can get angry. That is a truth that the Bible attests to, that God does get angry. He might be slow to anger, but he does get angry. There is part of us, if we are honest, that finds that quite uncomfortable. One of the real challenges that we have when we come to the Bible is that we tend to look at the Old Testament and think, *angry God*, and then look at the New Testament and think *nice Jesus*. However, this provides us with a real dilemma, because as we have already seen Jesus is the exact representation of God's nature. So, either we have misunderstood the God of the Old Testament, or Jesus in the New Testament, or both. Part of that comes when we view anger as a negative thing, which is very much our modern take on it. We don't like people who get angry because we don't always feel safe around them. Anger can often be linked to abusive situations and when we project that onto God, we get an uncomfortable image that is much easier to reject in favor of a nicer New Testament Jesus.

However, the scriptures do not have such a negative view of God's anger. He gets angry at evil, and injustice, and his anger burns against anything that would seek to limit the scope and impact of his love. He is angry when his people reject him, and he is angry when they live in the opposite way to the life he called them to. However, God's anger is always portrayed as a reaction or response to these situations rather than part of his nature. His nature that he reveals to Moses is that he is slow to anger. One of the many places that these wonderful words get repeated are Psalm 103:

---

18. Exod 34:6–7.

> "The Lord is compassionate and gracious,
>   slow to anger, abounding in love.
> He will not always accuse,
>   nor will he harbor his anger forever;
> he does not treat us as our sins deserve
>   or repay us according to our iniquities.
> For as high as the heavens are above the earth,
>   so great is his love for those who fear him;
> as far as the east is from the west,
>   so far has he removed our transgressions from us."[19]

So, God is patient with us beyond what we deserve, despite our rejection of him and his ways. That is who he is. That is the mark of his character. The people in biblical times took great comfort from the fact that God not only got angry but put boundaries around that anger. In other words, these are the circumstances when I'm going to be angry; but that anger isn't an instantaneous rage like the Incredible Hulk, and there is always a path back.

That can give us great comfort too in a world that at times has real evil and injustice in it. Who wants a God who doesn't get angry at evil? Who wants a God who is indifferent in the face of injustice?

The King James Version translates patience, and slow to anger in the same way: longsuffering. Even though that has slipped from our vocabulary these days, what is great about it is that it captures something of the consistency of God's character, and that is something important when it comes to understanding patience.

The gods of the cultures around Israel were capricious, and their anger or favor could be ignited with the smallest slight. You didn't know whether the gods would favor you one moment or destroy you the next. Knowing that there were circumstances when God could get angry, but that he was slow to anger and leaning always towards grace, compassion, faithfulness and love, gave you the stability of knowing that God was consistent even in an inconsistent world. That his nature, his character was consistent regardless of what is going on around him. He is responsive, yes, but consistent in his character and is therefore trustworthy.

---

19. Ps 103:8–12.

Patience with a purpose

So it is into this image that we are being transformed. We too are called to be consistent in our character while living in an inconsistent world. When there are those around us who treat us badly, or who get under our skin; we are called to live consistently in the image of Jesus. When we are going through hard times, even the hardest of times, we are called to live consistently in the image of Jesus.

The patience of God is a patience with a purpose. Peter reminds us:

> "The Lord is not slow in keeping his promise, as some understand slowness. Instead, he is *patient* with you, not wanting anyone to perish, but everyone to come to repentance."[20]

Patience is vital for healthy and restored relationships. Why is God patient with us? To bring us back into a relationship with him. Why are we called to be patient with others? So that we can maintain healthy relationships.

It is important that we don't confuse patience and tolerance, which is something that we are in danger of doing at times. It is possible to not tolerate behavior while at the same time being patient, being consistent in character even when the other person is being inconsistent. That's hard in a relationship, whether it's a spouse, family member, friend or colleague. I am so thankful that over the years my wife Bex has been patient with my inconsistencies; but she shouldn't have to tolerate them. The challenge is, which she does so well, to not tolerate them while remaining patient. What about you? Do you often fall into the trap of tolerating things that you shouldn't, all under the banner of patience? Is that the kind of patience God has with us? Does he tolerate our mistakes? Not at all. He paid the heavy price for our sin and rebellion, but he did so while being consistent in his character even while we were living inconsistently. He has been slow to anger. He has been patient. You do not have to tolerate sin and brokenness in your relationships to make yourself feel like you are being patient.

There is wisdom in knowing when to speak and when not to. We are not always patient in waiting for the right time to speak. Social media hasn't helped with that. So often if there is a conversation on a group on social media (and when I say conversation, read debate) I get sucked into it far too willingly. Commenting is just a few clicks away as I throw my two pence worth into the mix, and then usually regret it. If we are not careful then the same can happen to us in our "real world" conversations. It is far too easy

20. 2 Pet 3:9.

to throw comments out there without giving thought about timing or tone. We are losing the ability to hold our opinions and thoughts because we assume that everyone would be deeply blessed to hear them. Spoiler alert: they may not be! Paul reminds the Ephesians of the importance of patience in maintaining relationships:

> "Be completely humble and gentle; be *patient*, bearing with one another in love."[21]

To bear with someone, to be patient while not tolerating sinful or destructive behavior, we need the wisdom of the Holy Spirit. We cannot do this on our own, and often it is when we try to that we fall short. We need the transformation of heart to understand that there is a lot in our own lives that God is being patient with before we ever get to the person next to us. If God is being patient with me, then I can assume that God is being patient with them. If God is being patient with them, then perhaps I need to be too.

TENDING THE SOIL

What are the weeds that we need to remove from our garden to help the fruit of patience grow?

Expectation

I heard the phrase recently that "expectations are premeditated resentments." In other words when we have an expectation we are setting ourselves up for disappointment because there are times when those expectations aren't met.

There are some expectations that are healthy, good, and need to form part of the framework of our lives and walks of discipleship. Is it reasonable for me to expect that another believer will treat me well? Yes, I think it is fair to have that expectation. Is it fair to expect that your spouse will honor their wedding vows? Totally.

Usually though it isn't those expectations that are the issue, or the challenge to our patience with others. Usually, it is when our expectations, little or large, are unmet that patience can unravel. Or when we have unhealthy or unqualified expectations. When I expect that things will go the way that

---

21. Eph 4:2.

The Maker's Mark

I want them to, or that people will do things the way that I want. Most of us have these unconscious expectations floating around inside us and it is only when we stop and process our thoughts and emotions that we become aware of them. Sadly this usually happens after something has gone wrong.

The challenge with expectation is that it gives us very little room for patience, for bearing with others because we have already assigned them a role in us achieving our happiness of which they are usually totally unaware. Then when they fail to meet those expectations, the full weight of our disappointment falls on them, making it very hard for us to be patient, slow to anger, or consistent in our responses.

It should be easy for us to think of examples in our own lives where we have felt resentful toward people who did not live up to our expectations. What do you expect from the people around you? Are those expectations realistic and reasonable? Does the person know what those expectations are and are they happy to fulfil them?

What about more generally? I have an expectation that if I order a steak to be cooked medium at a restaurant it will not come out rare. When it's rare it practically still moos, so I expect that the chef will give me what I have ordered. Do we treat life like this in general? That I expect things to happen the way that I want them to? The problem then happens when life is not what we expect. Something unexpected comes along. We might have an expectation of happiness, but then we experience depression. We might have the expectation of fairytale love, but then someone breaks our hearts. We might have the expectation of wealth but then we lose our job. We might have the expectation of a long and healthy life, but then we get an unexpected diagnosis that changes everything.

People and life are unpredictable, and so we need to be wise with our expectations so that we can both bear with the inconsistencies of others, and bear under the inconsistencies of life.

Hurry

One of the big tests of patience is when we are in a rush. Odds are if you think of situations where you feel your patience is most threatened, a good deal of them will be when you are rushing or feeling rushed. For me, if it is usually when I am meant to be somewhere at a certain time, and something has come up that puts me behind.

How do you cope with hurry?

At the start of his helpful book *The Ruthless Elimination of Hurry*, John Mark Comer quotes psychologist Carl Jung:

"Hurry is not *of* the devil; hurry *is* the devil."[22]

It is often in those places of hurry that we rush ahead and leave ourselves and others behind. It is often when we rush ahead that we leave God behind, even while we are busy trying to live for him.

At the moment I am writing this chapter I am around two thirds of the way through a sabbatical, which I am blessed to be able to take every seven years. It lasts three months, where I step away from pastoral responsibility in the life of the church. It is a wonderful gift, a form of reset which allows space to stop and grow that is not always easy while leading a church. It has been such a blessing to rediscover patterns of life that so easily get lost among the busy and the hurry. Sometimes it is in the stopping that we can really evaluate what matters. When we are living out of an unhurried place, we have room to be patient, and to be responsive to others.

Patience notices. It notices a need in yourself and a need in others and has the freedom to respond as an act of love. When we are rushing it is hard to notice our needs or the needs of others, and so not only do we have less capacity for patience, and less time to give it, but we don't really see how and where to respond either.

You see we live in such a fast-paced world, where so much of what we do happens at a rapid pace. How many of the financial issues we face in our families and businesses across the country come about because people don't want to wait for the things they want. How many of the relationship issues in life, in marriages, in families, come about because there is a lack of bearing with one another in love? We need to slow down a little, slow down the pace of life. Be prepared to wait, don't always go for the instant results. Whatever happened to the phrase

"it's worth the wait?"

When we are hurried, we are less patient, less understanding, less present; we are more likely to lose our temper and snap. Rather than being slow to anger, we become like those capricious gods of the ancient world, maybe acting favorably and maybe smiting those around us. The one thing we are not is consistently like Jesus.

Jesus may not have taken a sabbatical or a retreat, but he did (as we have already seen) take time away to be with the Father. I am sure that this

---

22. Quoted in Comer, *Ruthless Elimination of Hurry*, 20.

contributed to his patience, and I am certain that if we look to eliminate hurry from our lives it will make us more patient too.

After all, God has been infinitely patient with us. Consistently showing faithful love to us when time and time again we get it wrong. Patience is who God is, it's his character. That's why it is part of the fruit of the Spirit.

Patience is the Makers mark.

QUESTIONS FOR REFLECTION

1. How much of a struggle is patience for you?
2. How can "God's timing" be a challenge to us?
3. How is Jesus' experience on the cross an example to us as we seek to grow patience in our lives?
4. Who are the people in your life who test your patience? Why?
5. Think of a time when you had to bear the weight of suffering. What helped you not lose patience?
6. Are you slow to anger or quick tempered?
7. What expectations in your life might be robbing you of patience?
8. Are there areas where you need to eliminate hurry to create space for patience?
9. How quickly will your life improve with a bit more patience? What shifts could occur in daily life with more patience that would bring about the joy we just discussed?

7

Kindness

IN MANY WAYS KINDNESS is one of the most underrated aspects of the fruit of the Spirit, and yet it is one that has a massive impact on our lives day by day.

Kindness is often undervalued. Yet many of us would be able to think of times in our lives when kindness has transformed the world for us.

The well-known theologian William Barclay once said, "more people have been brought into the church by the kindness of real Christian love than by all the theological arguments in the world."

How important is kindness? About twenty years ago I remember reading a study of forty cultures from around the world. There were sixteen thousand participants who were asked about their most desired traits in a partner. For both sexes, the first preference was *kindness*!

THE IMAGE OF JESUS

When it comes to Jesus it is often his kindness that draws people to him, both two thousand years ago, and today. In an interview online I saw recently, comedian and atheist Ricky Gervais said that what struck him about Jesus was his kindness. So many times, throughout the gospels it is the power of kindness in a cruel world that shines forth from Jesus. There are countless examples we could choose to explore, but I want to focus on just two.

The Maker's Mark

He sees me

Firstly, the healing of the bleeding woman in Luke's gospel:

> "And a woman was there who had been subject to bleeding for twelve years, but no one could heal her. She came up behind him and touched the edge of his cloak, and immediately her bleeding stopped.
>
> 'Who touched me?' Jesus asked.
>
> When they all denied it, Peter said, 'Master, the people are crowding and pressing against you.'
>
> But Jesus said, 'Someone touched me; I know that power has gone out from me.'
>
> Then the woman, seeing that she could not go unnoticed, came trembling and fell at his feet. In the presence of all the people, she told them why she had touched him and how she had been instantly healed. Then he said to her, 'Daughter, your faith has healed you. Go in peace.'"[1]

There are several things that strike me about the kindness of Jesus in this passage.

Let's start with the context. Jesus is not simply out and about on a stroll when we find him here in Luke 8, he is on the way to the house of Jairus to heal his daughter. A twelve-year-old girl is gravely sick, her father is rushing Jesus to be there in time to heal her, but Jesus stops. He stops for this woman. We don't even know her name.

What we are told though is that she has suffered from this illness that has caused bleeding for twelve years. For the whole time that Jairus' daughter has been alive this woman has suffered.

She has spent all that she has on doctors and none of them has been able to cure her. She is hopeless.

Because of her bleeding, under Jewish law she was unclean. She couldn't be touched, and everyone around her would have had to keep their distance. Friends, family and society would have rejected her.

By coming into this crowded place, and by touching Jesus she takes a massive risk. Touching Jesus, a man, as a woman was frowned upon. Touching someone else would have made them unclean too under the law.

She reaches out and touches the hem of his garment. What she touches are probably the tzitzit, the ritual prayer tassels that are on the edges of his robe. This dates all the way back to when the spies entered Canaan:

---

1. Luke 8:43-48; the account can also be found in Matt 9:20-22 and Mark 5:24-34.

> "Speak to the Israelites and say to them: 'Throughout the generations to come you are to make tassels on the corners of your garments, with a blue cord on each tassel.'"[2]

As she touches this fringe of his garment she is healed. Jesus feels the power go out from him and stops, asking "who touched me?" When the woman realizes she can't remain hidden any more, she comes forward and explains herself to Jesus.

What highlights the kindness of Jesus in this moment is that he doesn't see her as a problem or distraction. He notices her. He sees her. He doesn't treat her like the rest of the world; he treats her differently because he sees her differently.

As Jesus sends her on her way, restored and full of shalom, he calls her daughter. It's the only time in the gospels that Jesus calls someone by that name. Again, here is an act of kindness, that someone who hasn't been allowed to enjoy normal family relationships has been called daughter. He brings her back into relationship.

One of the amazing things is that this unknown woman, shunned by society, is the means through which a prophecy about Jesus is fulfilled. In Malachi we read:

> "But for you who revere my name the sun of righteousness shall rise, with healing in its wings. You shall go out leaping like calves from the stall."[3]

The word we have in the Hebrew for *wings* comes from the same root word that denotes the four corners of the garments which these fringes are on. So, as she comes into contact with the wings of the Son of righteousness, she is healed. It's a reversal of the normal process. In touching a person, she would have made them unclean, but Jesus can't be made unclean. Instead, as she touches him she is made clean, made whole, restored.

This story reminds me so much of the story of Hagar in the Old Testament which you can read about in Genesis 16. Hagar, like this woman, had seen mistreated and finds herself cast out from society. She is wandering in the wilderness and has an amazing encounter with God. She is given this amazing privilege of giving God a name, and the name she chooses is El Roi, "You are the God who sees me."[4]

2. Num 15:38.
3. Mal 4:2, *New Revised Standard Version*.
4. Gen 16:13.

God notices her when nobody else does.

That is the kindness of Jesus, that he stops to notice this woman. Even in the middle of a really pressing crowd, with the tension of Jarius and his concern for his daughter, Jesus stops to notice this daughter.

I wonder who the people are in the crowds of our lives, that the Lord wants us to stop and notice? Who are the people to whom we need to speak words of kindness? Who are the ones that we need to draw in and speak words of relationship to?

Cross over the road

The second example I want to focus on is from one of the most well-known parables of Jesus. When asked by a scribe what he had to do with inherit eternal life, Jesus asks him what his understanding of the law is. He replies by quoting Deuteronomy and Leviticus:[5]

> "'Love the Lord your God with all your heart and with all your soul and with all your strength and with all your mind'; and, 'Love your neighbor as yourself.'"[6]

The man then asks Jesus, "who is my neighbor?" This sets up the parable of the Good Samaritan.

> "In reply Jesus said: 'A man was going down from Jerusalem to Jericho, when he was attacked by robbers. They stripped him of his clothes, beat him and went away, leaving him half dead. A priest happened to be going down the same road, and when he saw the man, he passed by on the other side. So too, a Levite, when he came to the place and saw him, passed by on the other side. But a Samaritan, as he traveled, came where the man was; and when he saw him, he took pity on him. He went to him and bandaged his wounds, pouring on oil and wine. Then he put the man on his own donkey, brought him to an inn and took care of him. The next day he took out two denarii and gave them to the innkeeper. "Look after him," he said, "and when I return, I will reimburse you for any extra expense you may have."
>
> Which of these three do you think was a neighbor to the man who fell into the hands of robbers?'

---

5. See Deut 6:5 and Lev 19:18.
6. Luke 10:27.

The expert in the law replied, 'The one who had mercy on him.'"[7]

In many ways this is a parable of unexpected kindness. Those who were expected to help do not, and the one who nobody thought would help, did.

Let's think of the main characters who encounter the injured man in this story.

First, we have the priest. Priests in the time of Jesus would have been wealthy and part of the elite class. Many of them lived in Jericho and would go up to Jerusalem to perform their priestly duties in the temple. But because they were wealthy and important they weren't going to walk the seventeen miles between the two places, so the people who hear the parable would have assumed that the priest was riding. He has the means to help.

However, the priest had a problem—and let's be generous and say it was a genuine problem. The man was unconscious, so he didn't know if he was a Jew or a gentile. If he was a Jew, he had an obligation under the law to help. But he also couldn't be sure if the man was alive or dead.

If he was dead, then he risked becoming unclean and would not be able to perform his duties in the temple. If he had risked it and had been found out, then the other priests could have taken him outside the temple and beaten him to death with clubs.

This question of whether this man was a neighbor was a potentially costly question for the priest. In the end he decides it's just not worth the risk.

Next you have the Levite, who is the assistant to the priest.

If the priest has set a precedent, how could the assistant upstage his master? What would have happened if the Levite had ridden into town with the man that the priest had determined through his study of the law he was unable to help? It would be an insult to the priest.

In the end he went along with the crowd and kept walking by.

Lastly you have the Samaritan, the hero of the story. The listeners would have seen the hierarchy go down from priest, to Levite, and then they would have expected a Jewish lay person. That's the natural progression for them, so what was coming next was unthinkable as it explodes in the faces of Jesus' audience. The hero of the story is not Jewish, but a hated outsider. Think, Palestinian to a patriotic Israeli today.

It is the outsider, the hated foreigner who shows compassion, who is a neighbor. A neighbor, not just to those who are like him, from the same race and religion and creed, but reaching across those barriers to show kindness.

---

7. Luke 10:30–37.

The Maker's Mark

It also comes at great risk. Imagine a Samaritan man transporting a beaten and unconscious Jew into town? Think, Native American Indian carrying a beaten and unconscious cowboy into the saloon of the wild west. What would people have assumed had happened? Would he have been given the benefit of the doubt?

It's a big story, full of big questions, for one that takes less than a minute to tell.

Notice that the question from the start isn't answered at the end. Who is my neighbor?

The question that the parable fires back at us is—to whom should *I be* a neighbor?

How should I practice costly kindness? You see kindness is an action. As the poetic songwriter and author Michael Card puts it in his book *Inexpressible*:

> "It is loading wounded people onto donkeys, running to greet runaway children, forgiving enormous debts, paying someone who worked an hour as much as the ones who work all day, giving a party to those who can't pay you back."[8]

It is practical, it makes a difference, it notices those others overlook, it comes from unexpected places. To whom should I be a neighbor? To whom should I show this kindness?

We see the answer in the beautiful consistency of the life and teaching of Jesus: to *anyone* in need!

That can seem overwhelming, can't it? There is so much need in the world that we can find it difficult to know where we can make a difference, even to the point that we don't engage at all. It doesn't need to be overwhelming though because Jesus is able to make it personal. Who are the people and situations that God has put in your path each day to get involved with? Yes the problems of the world are important, but don't miss the simple need of kindness to a person you might come across today.

THE FRUIT OF KINDNESS

If we are called to bear the mark of the Maker in the world, to continue that transformative journey of becoming more like Jesus, then how do we look at kindness? How do we show kindness?

---

8. Card, *Inexpressible*, 116.

Hesed

Hesed is a word that we can translate different ways. That shouldn't surprise us; many words in both Hebrew and Greek are like that because we are spanning thousands of years across differing cultures. When it comes to hesed its more than culture and time, its depth. Hesed is a deep word, and that's why we often find it hard to translate. Words that translators have often fallen on are love, goodness, faithfulness, mercy, favor and kindness.

In many ways hesed is the combination of all of them because no one of them can quite contain all that hesed is doing.

Kindness in today's world doesn't seem like an especially deep word. It can be speaking a kind word or holding the door open for someone. Simple everyday acts. That's kindness, and it is absolutely the kindness that we as followers of Jesus should be practicing. The kindness we see revealed in the scriptures though goes far deeper than that, and that is where hesed is a challenge to us.

When God sends angels to warn Lot and his family about the coming destruction of Sodom, and the angels help them escape when they seem paralyzed with fear, Lot says that "they have shown great kindness in sparing my life."[9] The word Lot uses here is hesed, and in this instance it's far greater than simply holding the door open. It is gracious, loyal, favor expressed often to people who don't deserve it.

Remember in the last chapter we looked at how God reveals his character to Moses on the mountain, and we explored how God is slow to anger? Hesed is a continuation of that revelation of God's nature. Let's just remind ourselves of that verse:

> "And he passed in front of Moses, proclaiming, 'The Lord, the Lord, the compassionate and gracious God, slow to anger, abounding in *lovingkindness* and faithfulness.'"[10]

Hesed is a word that God uses to describe himself, and 75 percent of the time it is used in the scriptures it is used to describe something of the character of God.

It appears almost 250 times in the scriptures, and over half of those occurrences in the Psalms:

---

9. Gen 19:19.

10. Exod 34:6 (NIV will often translate *hesed* as "love," but here and after I have translated as *lovingkindness*).

The Maker's Mark

> "Your *lovingkindness*, Lord, reaches to the heavens,
>   your faithfulness to the skies."[11]

> "For as high as the heavens are above the earth,
>   so great is his *lovingkindness* for those who fear him."[12]

In just these two examples we see the immense height and depth of God's kindness.

Hesed is a covenant word. It is a word that is expressed in the context of relationship, but in a sense, it expresses the desire to go above and beyond what is expected to show the extent of lovingkindness.

When my grandmother was nearing the end of her life we made several trips to hospital to see her. My grandad was there, sitting by her side, as he had been for the 68 years that they had been married. He sang to her and held her hand. He smiled and he cried. It was a loyal love that fulfilled all the promises that he had made to her as they took their vows in 1955. If he had sat there from a distance and simply told her that he loved her, that wouldn't quite have been the same. Equally, there were nursing staff who were there with her over that time, but it was their job to care for her, so it wasn't simply being there that mattered either. It was the covenant relationship, in this case a marriage, which expressed all those words translators have wrestled with over the years, love, goodness, faithfulness, mercy, favor and kindness. Hesed!

What is it that the Psalmist is trying to convey? That Lovingkindness is the tone of God's actions towards us. When we hear the voice of the Father, or the words of the Son, or the whisper of the Spirit, it is *hesed* that we are hearing. It is the kindness of a God who stays with us,[13] and sings over us,[14] and takes us by the hand.[15] It is the kindness of God that not only reaches to the heavens, but through every year of your life.

I grew up listening to American singer/songwriter Michael Card. The poetic depth of his lyrics, and the beautiful melody of his music touched something deep in me growing up and does still to this day. I had the great joy of meeting Michael on his last trip to the UK and spent a few moments with him. Despite his music touching many around the world, he remains

---

11. Ps 36:5.
12. Ps 103:11.
13. See Isa 43:1–3.
14. See Zeph 3:17.
15. See Isa 41:13.

KINDNESS

a truly humble man. What has touched me in new ways in recent years has been the power of his writing, and I've already quoted from his book *Inexpressible* in this chapter. It is an insightful look into this word *hesed*, and the impact that it has on us.

In the chapter entitled "Gemilut Hesed and Tikkun Olam" Michael talks about how the according to the Talmud, the Torah begins and ends with *hesed*.[16]

It Genesis 3 after Adam and Eve have eaten the forbidden fruit, God clothes them. This is a profound act of kindness following on from his rejection by humanity. Their actions would bring sin and death into God's perfect world, setting off a chain of events that would eventually culminate in the cross; and yet God tenderly clothes them rather than allowing them to continue to live in shame.

At the end of the Torah, in Deuteronomy 34, God buries Moses. At the end of his life Moses is allowed to see the land that his people will enter, but he cannot. As he looks across at the land, knowing that the work the Lord had for him is finished, he died. I've said before that sometimes the simplicity of the words of scripture, or our familiarity with them can lessen their impact on us. This is one of those verses:

> "He buried him . . ."[17]

God buried Moses. He takes him down from the mountain, into the valley, and he buried him. What an extraordinary act of kindness from a God who mightily rescued his people through signs and wonders, parts the sea and leads them in a fiery cloudy pillar. This is a covenant act, not to a people group or even to its leader, but to a friend. That's the relationship described in Exodus:

> "The Lord would speak to Moses face to face, as one speaks to a friend."[18]

Who is it that lays a person to rest? It is family and friends, and in this act of kindness to a friend, this is the role taken on by the Lord.

---

16. See Card, *Inexpressible*, 130.
17. Deut 34:6.
18. Exod 33:11.

The Maker's Mark

What Use Is Kindness?

It is easy to think of that faithful, loyal love we see so fully expressed in God and to simply internalize it as a nice warm feeling towards others. The word that Paul uses for kindness in Galatians 5 comes from the root word that Strongs Bible Concordance translates to mean *usefulness*. That's quite helpful to us as we think about how we are to live out this fruit of the Spirit in our own lives. The danger we must avoid though is thinking that this is simply about being nice. Remember everything that we have looked at when it comes to hesed. There is a deep relational drive to our character and behavior, which spurs us on to action.

It is God who clothes Adam and Eve and buries Moses. That utterly relational drive of lovingkindness is expressed through action, and that must be true for us too, or what use is our kindness. What use is the expression of our sympathy to another if we are unwilling to do something to ease pain or provide comfort. What use is our kindness to a lonely person if it doesn't manifest in easing their loneliness.

Think about Jesus' teaching about the sheep and the goats in Matthew 25:

> "Then the King will say to those on his right, 'Come, you who are blessed by my Father; take your inheritance, the kingdom prepared for you since the creation of the world. For I was hungry and you gave me something to eat, I was thirsty and you gave me something to drink, I was a stranger and you invited me in, I needed clothes and you clothed me, I was ill and you looked after me, I was in prison and you came to visit me.'"[19]

In parallel the goats on the left are criticized for their lack of action.

What separates the sheep on the right and the goats on the left? It was kindness that expressed itself in action. It was food for the hungry, it was drink for the thirsty, it was welcome for the stranger, clothes for the naked, care for the sick and visits for the prisoner. It wasn't simply sympathy, or prayer, or correct theology. It was useful action.

When we do these things, as Jesus said even for the least of these, we do it for him. Our kindness expressed in actual acts is a care for Jesus himself. In contrast, our failure to act in kindness to the least around us is a failure to care for the Lord.

---

19. Matt 25:34–36.

How does your kindness express itself to others? Is it limited to sympathy? A warm fuzzy feeling? An offer to pray? Or is it lived out in practical and useful action that improves the lives of others?

Think back a moment to the parable of the good Samaritan. Luke 10:33 tells us that the Samaritan "took pity" on the wounded man. What form did that pity take? Kindness. We read about what form this kindness took as the passage continues. He bandages his wounds, he puts him on a donkey, and he cares for him. He doesn't run and alert the authorities and get someone else to do it.

We once looked at this parable in a café church setting, with discussion and questions around the tables, and somebody fed back in that the parable highlighted how we can outsource care because the Samaritan paid the innkeeper to look after the wounded man. Yes the Samaritan did give money to the innkeeper to provide care, but there are a couple of things within that we need to consider.

Firstly, the Samaritan had already provided costly and risk-filled care to the man long before he reaches the inn.

Secondly, the giving of the moment was not a handing over of responsibility, rather a cementing of it with the promise of meeting any further costs upon return.

There may be times when additional or professional help is needed to provide care, but that should never be a reason for us not to provide the practical care we can to those in need as an expression of kindness.

David and Mephibosheth

In my previous book *After God's Heart*, I devoted a whole chapter to the story of David and Mephibosheth. It is a powerful story which has hesed, practical kindness right at the heart.

You can read about this story in 2 Samuel 9.

Some of you will remember that David was very good friends with King Saul's son Jonathan, and Mephibosheth was Jonathan's son. Both Saul and Jonathan are killed in a battle with the Philistines, and this filled the rest of Saul's family with terror. What usually happened when a new King came to the throne was that they would kill all the male family members of the old king so that there wouldn't be anyone left to challenge their claim the throne. According to this custom, Mephibosheth could have been in very real danger.

He goes into hiding in a place called *Lo Debar*, which means, the place of forgetting: this was a person who for many reasons did not want to be found.

However, he is eventually brough before King David. Can you imagine what he was thinking? What does he believe is coming next? Suffering from an injury he sustained as a child, unable to walk, he painfully bows down in homage and asks:

> "What is your servant, that you should notice a dead dog like me?"

It shows you something of how he sees himself, but also how he wants David to see him. He doesn't want David to see him as a threat. He doesn't want David to see him as a member for the former royal family or a princely grandson of the late King Saul. It's better for David to see him as he sees himself, as a dead dog.

How David responds in this moment gives us a glimpse into why he is a man after God's heart:

> "'Don't be afraid,' David said to him, 'for I will surely show you *lovingkindness* for the sake of your father Jonathan. I will restore to you all the land that belonged to your grandfather Saul, and you will always eat at my table.'"[20]

What does David show Mephibosheth? It's that word again: *hesed*. Loving kindness, and again its expressed practically. It is the returning of lands and a place at the table.

There are two further things that are worth noticing about the kindness that David shows in this story.

Firstly, it is deliberate, and we see that right at the start of the chapter:

> "David asked, 'Is there anyone still left of the house of Saul to whom I can show *lovingkindness* for Jonathan's sake?'"[21]

Before he even knows of Mephibosheth, David's desire is to show kindness. His love for Jonathan motivates him to reach out in some way in acts of kindness.

This is a challenge for us. Are we looking to show kindness? Do we believe that acts of kindness to others are an important part of our discipleship, of our bearing the Maker's mark in the world, so we go looking for those on whom we can lavish kindness?

20. 2 Sam 9:7.
21. 2 Sam 9:1.

Secondly, this kindness brought a change in how Mephibosheth was seen. He saw himself as a dead dog, useless, worthless, and of no threat, and as we have already seen, that's how he wanted David to see him too. However, the love that David had for Jonathan, and the desire to show hesed, lovingkindness, lifted Mephibosheth's status in David's eyes and consequently in his own eyes too. The forgotten one had been remembered. The outcast had been given a seat at the table. The one who had been bowed low in shame was now lifted in honor.

When we show kindness to others, it changes the way that we see them, and it can change the way that they see themselves too.

The mother of the prophet Samuel, Hannah, praises God:

> "He raises the poor from the dust
>   and lifts the needy from the ash heap;
> he seats them with princes
>   and makes them inherit a throne of honor."[22]

That's what we see in the kindness shown to Mephibosheth; lifted from the ashes to be seated with princes.

That's what we see with the good Samaritan, lifted from the dust of public opinion and social convention to be honored in the sight of generations.

This is the kindness we see in God himself, who rescues us and lifts us out of the dust of our own brokenness, and seats us at the table of his Son. The God who created all that is, who sustains it all through the word of his mouth; is kind. Michael Card wonders with us:

> "It is difficult for us to imagine how a being who is infinite in power submerses that power in kindness."[23]

As with all these different parts of the fruit of the Spirit, we do not bear the makers mark perfectly, or as consistently as we would like. Our character is still being formed and shaped into the likeness of Jesus. However, as we look at the scriptures, and we follow the ones in whose image we are made, it is made simple for us:

> "He has shown you, O mortal, what is good.
>   And what does the Lord require of you?
> To act justly and to love *lovingkindness*

---

22. 1 Sam 2:8.
23. Card, *Inexpressible*, 36.

and to walk humbly with your God."[24]

TENDING THE SOIL

Think back to chapter 3, how indifference and self-centeredness hinder the growth of love. They are certainly weeds for kindness too. However, as we end this chapter I want to focus on where there verse above from Micah finishes: walking humbly, or in this case the opposite: pride.

If there is a weed that stops the fruit of kindness from being grown in our lives, then it is pride. As we over value ourselves, we end up devaluing others.

A story that illustrates this well is one that Jesus himself tells in Luke 18, about a Pharisee and a tax collector.

> "To some who were confident of their own righteousness and looked down on everyone else, Jesus told this parable: 'Two men went up to the temple to pray, one a Pharisee and the other a tax collector. The Pharisee stood by himself and prayed: "God, I thank you that I am not like other people—robbers, evildoers, adulterers—or even like this tax collector. I fast twice a week and give a tenth of all I get."

But the tax collector stood at a distance. He would not even look up to heaven, but beat his breast and said, "God, have mercy on me, a sinner."'

> I tell you that this man, rather than the other, went home justified before God. For all those who exalt themselves will be humbled, and those who humble themselves will be exalted."[25]

In today's culture we do not think of pride as something terrible. We are encouraged to take pride in ourselves, to take pride in our work and achievements, so that we can build a healthy and robust sense of self-worth. This has been one of the legacies of psychological development over the past century. However, it is important to realize that there is a healthy sense of pride as well as an unhealthy one.

An example of healthy pride would be when we look at God's act of creation. Each day he pauses, looks out on the world that he has made and

---

24. Mic 6:8.
25. Luke 18:9–14.

declares "it is good." There is pride in the work he has done, and in the beauty and goodness of what he has made.

What we see here with the Pharisee though is unhealthy pride. Not only does he exalt himself, to use the NIV translator's word, but by doing so he puts the tax collector down. That is one of the ugliest parts of pride, of a puffed-up ego; that for you to be lifted you must stand on someone else. To have a puffed-up view of your own intelligence, you need to highlight someone who is less intelligent. To feel puffed up about your own achievements or status, you need to highlight the lesser achievements or status of others. You might not do it verbally, or even consciously, but often it is there deep in our hearts. The Pharisee gives voice to those puffed-up inner parts of our lives: "God, I thank you that I am not like other people . . ."

To lift himself up, he puts the tax collector, as well as a host of others, down.

With an increase in psychological tolerance and freedom there needs to come a higher level of emotional intelligence and spiritual self-awareness. We need to understand the motives of our hearts as we seek to weed out unhealthy pride. Why is it that pride is such a treat to the fruit of kindness in our lives? In a very real sense unhealthy pride, or being puffed-up, is taking up too much space, and when we take up too much space then there isn't enough room for others. When we take up too much space, whether we mean it or not, we take space away from others.

Humility is taking up the right amount of space which allows others to do the same. Pride creates barriers to empathy and compassion which are crucial to our relationships with others, but humility, seeing ourselves in the right light, allows us to connect with others.

We need to be honest with ourselves before God to root out the weed of pride from our lives. When I understand that I make mistakes, that I get things wrong, that I am as dependent on grace as anyone else, I look at others with a greater sense of compassion and kindness. I am kind to them because I know that God has been kind to me. When I know that I have been lifted from rock bottom by God, I have the desire to see others lifted and to actively participate in that lifting.

To put it simply, you can't be kind to some if you are proud. It is a weed that we need to work at removing from the garden of our hearts, because doing so softens the ground, allowing the tender fruit of kindness to grow.

Kindness is the Maker's mark.

QUESTIONS FOR REFLECTION

1. What is your favorite story of kindness in the life of Jesus?
2. Who are the people you can notice and pay attention to as an act of kindness?
3. Are there those it would be costly for you to show kindness to?
4. What are some of the ways you have experienced the lovingkindness of God?
5. Is your kindness useful to others?
6. What are some examples of healthy and unhealthy pride in your life?
7. What barriers are there to the Pharisee being kind to the tax collector?
8. Are there areas of your life where you need to take up less space as an act of kindness to others?

8

Goodness

ARE YOU A GOOD person?

When I speak to people about their spiritual lives, especially those who aren't following Jesus, this is usually their fallback phrase; "I'm a good person." What is it that they mean by that? What is the goodness they are referring to? Sometimes is not about the specific presence of anything good, but rather an absence of something terrible, in other words "I'm not a bad person!"

Is that what we are talking about when we think about the fruit of Goodness? The presence of certain "good" acts and the absence of the specific "bad" acts? That seems a little two-dimensional to me, so I would like to suggest that there is something deeper going on as we explore this fruit together.

THE IMAGE OF JESUS

Despite his response to the rich ruler, "why do you call me good, no-one is good except God alone,"[1] we think of Jesus as the walking, talking, embodiment of goodness. As we attempt to put some flesh on the bones of this fruit, there are two examples from Jesus' life and teaching that I want to focus on.

The first we read about in Matthew 20 when Jesus tells the parable of the workers in the vineyard. It is a story about a landowner who wants to

---

1. See Luke 18:18–19.

The Maker's Mark

hire workers to work in his vineyard. Having hired an initial group early in the morning, agreeing to pay them a denarius, he then goes at 9am, noon, 3pm and 5pm to hire more workers so that the work will be done on time.

When the time comes for the workers to be paid their wages, the landowner comes first to those who were hired last, paying them a denarius. You can imagine the thinking of those who had worked all day, "if he's paid those guys a denarius for just a couple of hours work, then we must be due a whole lot more because we have worked all day!" But they are bitterly disappointed when it comes to their turn and they receive the denarius they were promised, just like the others. So they start to grumble! Wouldn't you and I? One of the biggest causes of our discontent and grumbles is unmet expectations.

> "But he answered one of them, 'I am not being unfair to you, friend. Didn't you agree to work for a denarius? Take your pay and go. I want to give the one who was hired last the same as I gave you. Don't I have the right to do what I want with my own money? Or are you envious because I am generous?'
> So the last will be first, and the first will be last."[2]

What has this parable got to do with the fruit of goodness? The word that Jesus used in the mouth of the landowner in that poignant line "are you envious because I am *generous*" is the same word the Paul used in Galatians 5 for "goodness" as the fruit if the Spirit.

Are you envious because I am *good*?

How do we define the goodness of Jesus based on the words of this parable? As Philip Yancey says in his book *What's So Amazing About Grace*, "Jesus' story makes no economic sense, and that was his intent."[3]

There is a lavish generosity to the landowner in the parable which is reflective of the lavish generosity within the heart of God. The parable is not a story about fair wages but about the lavish generosity of God. Thank the Lord that I do not get paid what I deserve, and that I don't get the consequences of my feeble attempts at being "good enough." I am utterly and totally reliant upon the generous goodness of God. I am often comforted by the verse I was given at my baptism:

> "See what great love the Father has *lavished* on us, that we should be called children of God!"[4]

---

2. Matt 20:13–16.
3. Yancey, *What's So Amazing About Grace*, 61.
4. 1 John 3:1.

Is this love dished out like some sort of performance-based pay? A reward for our righteousness? No, it is lavished upon us, poured out towards us from the overflowing fulness of love that resides in the heart of the Father towards his children. We cannot earn it or disqualify ourselves from it; we can only receive it as a child receives a gift.

The nature of this goodness in the parable is important to understand. It is not what is expected, but it goes far beyond it. That is the nature of Grace. It is not the expected response, or even the acceptable response. It is offensive to the religious bean-counters and those who feel as though they deserve it. To those who know their need for it, who understand that they have no hope on their own of receiving it, it is the very air we breathe.

One of the biggest challenges that people must overcome in coming to faith in Jesus is the belief in their own goodness. When we think we are "good enough," then we fail to recognize our need to be rescued. God's goodness is a stark challenge to us because in acknowledging that God alone is good, we must admit that we are not, and that we need rescuing.

That leads me on to the second example of goodness in the life and ministry of Jesus.

In John 10 Jesus describes himself as the Good Shepherd:

> "I am the good shepherd. The good shepherd lays down his life for the sheep. The hired hand is not the shepherd and does not own the sheep. So when he sees the wolf coming, he abandons the sheep and runs away. Then the wolf attacks the flock and scatters it. The man runs away because he is a hired hand and cares nothing for the sheep."[5]

I love John's gospel, and it is here that we see the seven *I am* sayings of Jesus, which includes *I am the good shepherd*.

The image of the shepherd is one which would have been familiar to the people of Jesus day. While shepherds were looked down upon by the religious and social elite, they had an important role within their culture.

For us to understand the role of a shepherd it's worth highlighting something important about sheep:

They are utterly defenseless and totally dependent upon the shepherd.

They have no ability to protect themselves from predators, they have a habit of getting themselves into trouble because they wander off. Flash floods caused by heavy rainfall could sweep them away, or bandits could steal them, or wolves, lions and bears could attack them. They are totally

---

5. John 10:11–13.

in need of a shepherd to survive. The role of a shepherd was vocational, because it was a tough job with great risk.

What makes Jesus the *good* shepherd? It is that he lays down his life. He goes beyond what the hired hand would do. A hired hand would look after and lead the sheep, but when the dangers come he will run away. Jesus goes beyond what others would do, laying down his life for his sheep.

The goodness of God, which is often the focus of our worship and praise at church, goes far beyond what we could expect or deserve.

Many years ago, I was visiting a friend who was working in London, so I got the train from where I lived to London Waterloo station. The journey took about an hour and a half. It was a cold afternoon, and the plan was to meet her for dinner near the station. As I walked into the main concourse of the station, I saw a homeless man sat asking for money. I didn't have any money that I could give, but then a though entered my head, and once it was there I couldn't shake it. I have a coat. Have you ever had one of those thoughts where you know, once it's in your head it's not going to go until you act upon it? It was one of those moments. What good is it if I say to this man, sorry I don't have any money, but I hope you keep warm, when I have a coat I could give him. I have several coats at home.

So, I gave the man my coat and carried on having a great evening with my friend.

Why am I telling you this story? It certainly isn't to make me look good, because sadly I can tell you I have walked past many cold and hungry people and not responded. This was a moment that had never happened before, and in the same way hasn't happened since.

The reason I share it is because, in that moment I realized that the goodness of God we are called to carry into the world is lived out in going beyond what is expected. It is extravagant, lavish and at times unexplainable. But it is good news to the hungry and the hurting, it is company to the lonely and solidarity to the marginalized. It is justice for the forgotten, mercy for those who deserve none, humility in the face of a proud and puffed-up world. And on that night, it was a coat for a cold man.

There are other examples we could explore together but these two already give us a picture of the extravagant and gracious nature of Jesus shaped goodness. In this next section we will move on to explore what this fruit can look like in our lives.

THE FRUIT OF GOODNESS

As we have already seen, the fruit of goodness is not just "doing" good things.

That's often the definition we give to it . . . good behavior. The reason why it must be more than that is that by that measure, everyone would have to be considered a good person. Even the worst of people, at the worst of times, is still capable of doing good things.

Like Kindness in the previous chapter, it is something that must be lived out in our lives in that it must have some use or benefit to others.

We see that in the way that goodness is spoken about in the New Testament.

When teaching about the difference between true and false prophets in Matthew 7 Jesus says:

> "By their fruit you will recognize them. Do people pick grapes from thornbushes, or figs from thistles? Likewise, *every good tree bears good fruit*, but a bad tree bears bad fruit. A good tree cannot bear bad fruit, and a bad tree cannot bear good fruit. Every tree that does not bear good fruit is cut down and thrown into the fire. Thus, by their fruit you will recognize them."[6]

There is productiveness about goodness. It is a short passage very much at the heart of what we have been exploring. A good tree bears the mark of good fruit. A person with character shaped like Jesus will bear the Makers mark, and their life will take on, in every increasing measure, the likeness of Jesus. That's the journey we are on.

Is your character producing good things? Trees will go through periods of greater and lesser productivity, and the same will be true for the fruits in our lives. So don't be discouraged if you aren't yet yielding the bumper crop of goodness for which you are hoping. However, if we produce bad fruit, then there's a problem that needs to be addressed. Something isn't right. We will come on to explore that in just a moment.

Think about Jesus telling the parable of the Sower in Luke 8:

> "Still other seed fell on *good* soil. It came up and yielded a crop, a hundred times more than was sown."[7]

---

6. Matt 7:16–20.
7. Luke 8:8a.

The Maker's Mark

There is a fertileness about goodness. Not only is it what our characters produce when we are living Jesus shaped and Spirit filled lives, but it is the environment through which other things can grow.

As we have already seen in the parable of the workers in the vineyard, there is a generosity in goodness.

This is biblical goodness. Not simply right behavior, or the absence of bad behavior, but a productive, fertile, generous spirit that bears fruit that nourishes and blesses others.

Jesus teaches us in Luke 6 that "a good man brings good things out of the good stored up in his heart, and an evil man brings evil things out of the evil stored up in his heart."[8]

The reason why there is goodness in us is because Jesus lives in us through his Spirit.

How do we express that in our day-to-day lives?

This is what the prophet Micah spells out to the people of God in the Old Testament.

> "With what shall I come before the Lord,
>   and bow myself before God on high?
> Shall I come before him with burnt offerings,
>   with calves a year old?
> Will the Lord be pleased with thousands of rams,
>   with ten thousands of rivers of oil?
> Shall I give my firstborn for my transgression,
>   the fruit of my body for the sin of my soul?"
> He has told you, O mortal, *what is good*;
>   and what does the Lord require of you
> but to do justice, and to love mercy,
>   and to walk humbly with your God?"[9]

Goodness must be expressed far beyond mere religious observance.

It isn't in the offerings they make, or the praise they offer, or their religious devotion. At least it is not only in those things. The goodness that God requires goes far beyond that, being lived out through the expression of justice, mercy and humility.

Someone put it like this . . . God wants spiritual fruit, not religious nuts.

I have been the pastor of churches for almost two decades, and there are occasions when I speak with people and wonder whether the leap has

---

8. Luke 6:45.
9. Mic 6:6–8.

been made between religious observance and living a spirit-filled life that bears the fruit of goodness. There can be those who know all the right prayers, sing the hymns and songs with full voice, who have come week in week out for many years; they give, they are interested, and their lives are invested in the church. But when I look at their lives, and when I see their hearts, I wonder how much transformation has taken place? Am I confident of that in my own life? How much is any goodness in me springing up from a transformed heart, or simply going through the motions?

Why should our lives bear this fruit of goodness? Because it is the Makers mark! We follow a God who is good, and who cares deeply about these things. As I've ready said, we can be good because the One living within us is good. We see that throughout the scriptures.

I've already mentioned that one of my favorite passages of the Bible growing up was the opening part of Psalm 107. As I have got older these words have come to take on a deeper meaning for me.

Let's just recap the first 9 verses:

> "Give thanks to the Lord, for he is good;
> his love endures forever.
> Let the redeemed of the Lord tell their story—
> those he redeemed from the hand of the foe,
> those he gathered from the lands,
> from east and west, from north and south.
> Some wandered in desert wastelands,
> finding no way to a city where they could settle.
> They were hungry and thirsty,
> and their lives ebbed away.
> Then they cried out to the Lord in their trouble,
> and he delivered them from their distress.
> He led them by a straight way
> to a city where they could settle.
> Let them give thanks to the Lord for his unfailing love
> and his wonderful deeds for humankind,
> for he satisfies the thirsty
> and fills the hungry with good things."[10]

God's goodness is constant, unwavering, and shown through his grace, mercy, and justice. That's why his desire for us is to go beyond religious observance, and into whole life devotion. That's what he does for us. "Let the redeemed of the Lord tell their story" says the Psalmist. What's the story?

10. Ps 107:1–9.

That he gathered, rescued and redeemed them. He settled them, nourished and provided for them.

Goodness . . . this is goodness.

It is the fruit of the Spirit on which even the poorest around us can feast.

It is the fertile ground in which humility flourishes.

It is the generous action of justice, fairness, and mercy to shape a better world.

This kind of goodness is essential in our life in Christ.

It might sound strange to explicitly say that those who follow Jesus should be good, but sadly it is not always the case. As I think back to the start of the chapter, it isn't simply the absence of bad behavior, but a life lived in response to deep heart transformation that is required. We were created in Christ to do good works.

When Paul writes to the Ephesians he reminds them:

> "For we are God's handiwork, created in Christ Jesus to do *good works*, which God prepared in advance for us to do."[11]

When a person gives their life to Jesus and commits to follow him, they are saved. However, we risk presenting that salvation as a little one dimensional if it is simply viewed as an escape from Hell. A cosmic "Get Out of Jail Free" card. It isn't just what we have been saved *from*, but what we are saved *for*. We are saved to spend eternity in the presence of the God who created and loves us . . . yes. But we are also saved for a purpose here and now, and that is for the good work that God has for us to do.

And that's why we call the gospel *good news*. Because we believe that it is rooted in the justice, mercy, love and compassion of God; and that it is lived out by his people to those around them in a way the blesses and enriches and transforms and liberates. When we join our will to God's word then amazing things can happen.

This is the work that God calls us to. To be ambassadors of the Kingdom of God. To not just be messengers of good news, but to be those who work and live out in our actions and our lives, the values of the Kingdom and the character of the King.

Focusing on Jesus does not distract us from a life of serving others, but rather it informs it. As Dallas Willard said:

---

11. Eph 2:10.

"Our inward turning towards God allows us to turn toward others."[12]

Jesus lived a life full of goodness, and so when we focus on him we are empowered to live that same goodness out in the world.

Towards the end of the New Testament John says:

> "Dear friend, do not imitate what is evil but what is good. Anyone who does what is good is from God. Anyone who does what is evil has not seen God."[13]

The Bible tells us to think about, to focus on, to seek to imitate that which is good. And we know that the things we seek to imitate will set the agenda for our lives.

Paul tells the early church to imitate him as he imitates Christ, which is an in-direct way of saying—imitate Christ—and a hopeful prayer that others may be encouraged to do so by his life.

You have the potential to be the greatest advertisement or the biggest warning to what a life centered on the character of Jesus is like. If others looked at your character, and the way you seek to imitate Christ . . . and imitated you . . . would they get to Christ? When others look at you, is it Christ that they see?

Are the things that you do for God motivated by religion or by the goodness of God lived out in your life to the blessing of others?

Does your character bear spiritual fruit . . . or are you a religious nut?

When we look at Christ we see the goodness of God, given freely for us.

We are called to have character like Jesus. To bear the Makers mark. That means that we are to try to imitate Christ as much as we can. God is transforming you into and conforming you to the image of Jesus—that's the goal of a disciple . . . to become more like the one they follow.

TENDING THE SOIL

What is it that would be a threat to the fruit of goodness growing in our lives?

If we are to focus on the words of Jesus in Matthew 7, that we are recognized by our fruit and that this comes from deep inside us, then we need to be honest about the state of our hearts and the state of our behavior.

---

12. Willard, *Scandal of the Kingdom*, 48.
13. 3 John 1:11.

The Maker's Mark

Remember, it is not simply about "good behavior," but nonetheless behavior can be a good indicator towards the state of our hearts.

Paul writes right before he speaks about the fruit of the Spirit:

> "The acts of the flesh are obvious: sexual immorality, impurity and debauchery; idolatry and witchcraft; hatred, discord, jealousy, fits of rage, selfish ambition, dissensions, factions and envy; drunkenness, orgies, and the like. I warn you, as I did before, that those who live like this will not inherit the kingdom of God."[14]

Or as Paul says to the Ephesians:

> "Get rid of all bitterness, rage and anger, brawling and slander, along with every form of malice."[15]

We all make mistakes. However, these actions are indicative of a much deeper issue within our hearts that presents a real challenge to the fruit of goodness being borne in our characters. Has there been a transformation? Have we prayed, not just once, but many times the prayer that David prayed:

> "Create in me a clean heart O God, and renew a right spirit within me."[16]

What is in us has a direct effect on what comes out of us. So, if we see the kind of actions that Paul lists here in Galatians 5 and Ephesians 4, it is not simply bad behavior, but it is unhealthy fruit coming from an unhealthy heart. That is why Paul pleads with us to *get rid* of it. It is no good for us.

Sometimes when working in the garden you need to know how healthy the soil is. You might test the soil to know whether you can plant it. Sometimes there might be chemicals present, or too much acidity in the soil. Sometimes the soil is too hard and needs to be softened. When we become observant about the state of our hearts, noting whether they have become bitter or hard, we will know whether what we hope to be planted in us stands a chance to grow or not. Sometimes it can be hard to spot. Dirt looks like dirt, right? So, you might need help, you might need to send it off to be tested by someone else, someone to partner with you in the process of creating the right conditions for growth.

What about the people around you? Your family and friends. Often, they are experts in the healthiness of the soil of your heart. They will often

---

14. Gal 5:19–21.
15. Eph 4:31.
16. Ps 51:10, *King James Version*.

notice, before you will, the unhealthy habits that are springing up in your life; the weeds that can choke the fruit of goodness from growing in you.

So, make yourself accountable to others and don't be afraid to ask the hard questions of yourself. If you aren't seeing the fruit of goodness growing in you, and what you see in its place are far less healthy things, then don't be afraid to explore those things.

There is an ancient practice in the life of the church called the Examen. Many people have practiced this method of prayerful reflection over the years, and it is still a practice that helps people tend the soil of their hearts today. There are several variations, but the version that was used by St Ignatius included these steps:

- Become aware of God's presence.
- Review the day with gratitude.
- Pay attention to your emotions.
- Choose one feature of the day and pray from it.
- Look toward tomorrow.

This pattern of reflective prayer can be a valuable tool in helping us to develop character shaped like Jesus. It helps us to identify what is good as well as what is unhealthy in our lives. We can then begin the prayerful yet deliberate process of weeding out that which is not good. As Paul says to the Romans:

"Hate what is evil, cling to what is good."[17]

One of the most amazing things I get to do as a pastor is to marry couples. It is an amazing joy to stand with a couple who are starting their married life together, to pray God's blessing on them and to share in this precious moment. It was a particular joy for me many years ago to stand alongside my sister and her husband as they started that journey together.

One of the things that I sometimes say to couples as they are beginning their life together is that marriage is a lot like an empty box. I know that sounds a bit bleak but bear with me. What I mean by that is that you can only take out of it what you put into it. What you put into your marriage matters. What you put into your relationship with your kids matters. What you put into your friendships matters. Why? Because what you put in will find its way out, and that is true for the better or worse, for good or bad.

17. Rom 12:9.

The Maker's Mark

That is certainly a rule for our hearts. What we put in will determine what comes out.

The talk that we listen to from those around us. The television shows we watch or the internet websites we browse. The books we read, and the advice take. Who we follow on social media. All of it was an effect on our lives, shapes our character and therefore determines the shape our actions and lives take.

That is why it is so important that we pay attention to what goes into our hearts and minds. Paul encourages the Philippians in this way:

> "Finally, brothers and sisters, whatever is true, whatever is noble, whatever is right, whatever is pure, whatever is lovely, whatever is admirable—if anything is excellent or praiseworthy—think about such things."[18]

Within each of us we have light and dark, good and bad. There is a battle raging constantly within us, as Paul says, between the good we want to do and the evil we do not want to do but keep on doing.[19]

There is an old Native American story of a grandfather who tells his grandson that there is a battle raging inside him between a good wolf and a bad wolf. The grandson is, understandably, worried and asks his grandfather which wolf will win the battle. The grandfather wisely replies, "whichever one you feed!"

What we are feeding determines our fruitfulness because we are either nurturing the soil of our character or we are poisoning it. We are either breaking up the soil so that it is healthy, allowing us to set down deep roots that will produce the fruit of goodness; or we allow the ground to be hard and shallow, producing a small and withered crop.

How are you tending the ground in your life? Are you making sure that you protect what is coming out of your life by guarding what goes in?

In Mark 11 we read about the story of Jesus and the fig tree. Jesus comes looking for fruit and he didn't find any so he declared that the tree would be barren forever. Despite all the hype of the crowd's welcome on Palm Sunday, and all the religion of the temple; Jesus came looking for fruit, to see if the people of God had got it, really got who they were supposed to be. What he found was that they hadn't got it, they had missed the opportunity to bear the Markers mark that they were always meant to bear to the world.

---

18. Phil 4:8.
19. See Rom 7:19.

So, while we struggle with the action of Jesus in cursing the tree, what we see is a prophetic judgment on the tree, which is symbolic of the human heart that just doesn't grow deeply enough to produce the fruit of the Kingdom.

Wonderfully, the journey into Jerusalem at the start of chapter 11 started at Bethphage, which ironically in Hebrew means the house of little figs. The soil wasn't deep enough here to produce good healthy trees that bore good fruit.

Because of the religious and legalistic systems of those who obeyed the letter of the law but no longer bore the Maker's mark, God's people had become a house of little figs. They were the trees producing withered and underdeveloped fruit because they were too shallow to grow properly. Right at the heart of this unhealthy orchard is the temple—which had become the opposite of why God gave it. Jesus goes on to say in verse 23:

> "Truly I tell you, if you have faith and do not doubt, not only can you do what was done to the fig tree, but also you can say to this mountain, 'Go, throw yourself into the sea,' and it will be done."[20]

We might think—how strange to throw in some teaching on prayer into this strange moment of the withering fig tree, but again I don't think that this what Jesus is saying, or at least I think what Jesus is saying is much more focused, much more linked to what we have just seen than that. The area where Jesus was speaking was just on top of the mount of olives, which looked over the temple, and the only mountain in sight was . . . the temple mount. When Jesus talks about "this mountain" the most central mountain in the life of the nation, the temple mount, being thrown into the sea then again this should be seen as a judgement of Jesus on the old ways of religious legalism—when we are "good people" without good works. When we are fruitful trees that no longer produce fruit.

The account of the withering of the fig tree, ironically, has deep roots. It is both an inspiration and a challenge to us today. It is an inspiration to us to bear fruit, but a challenge and a warning for us if we do not.

Jesus has already told us what happens when we don't bear the fruit he is looking for:

> "A man had a fig tree growing in his vineyard, and he went to look for fruit on it but did not find any. So, he said to the man who took care of the vineyard, 'For three years now I've been coming to look

---

20. Mark 11:23.

for fruit on this fig tree and haven't found any. Cut it down! Why should it use up the soil?'"[21]

As Donald Bridge reflects in his wonderful book *Travelling Through the Promised Land*:

> "God's Judgement, so often, is simply to say, 'very well, go the way of your own choice—be what you want to be,' with all the inevitable consequences of such a choice."[22]

At the end of the day we can say the right things, the right words of welcome as Jesus approaches. We can be in the right place, the places God has given for prayer and worship; but if we do not express the heart of God, if we do not bear the fruit of goodness, if we do not bear the Maker's Mark; then we are like this tree: shallow and with nothing to really show for our existence.

The Lord is coming, approaching our tree in search of fruit—should we feel excited, or should we be worried?

Goodness is the Maker's mark.

QUESTIONS FOR REFLECTION

1. Would you describe yourself as a "good person?"
2. When people refer to themselves as "good people," what qualities are they referring to?
3. Is your goodness reflective of the extravagance of the landowner in Matthew 20?
4. In what ways could you "go further" in doing good?
5. What are the good works that God has prepared for us to do?
6. Why is it easier to focus on our productivity (what comes out) instead of the state of our hearts?
7. Are there any tools like the Examen which help you to reflect on the health of your character?
8. What are you "putting into" your life so that what comes out is healthy?
9. Are you bearing the healthy fruit that Jesus is looking for?

---

21. Luke 13:6–7.
22. Bridge, *Travelling Through the Promised Land*, 126.

9

Faithfulness

I REMEMBER YEARS AGO reading a story that went something like this.

In America there is an air force base in Nevada that is known as Area 51. It's where, allegedly, all the top-secret stuff is kept that the American government doesn't want anyone else to know about. Late one afternoon the personnel who worked there were very surprised when a small private plane landed at their *secret* base. They immediately impounded the plane and hauled the pilot off for questioning.

The pilot explained that he had just taken off from Las Vegas, gotten lost and then spotted the base just as he was running out of fuel. The air force started a full background check with the FBI and held the pilot overnight during the investigation. By the next day they were finally convinced that he really had gotten lost and that he wasn't a spy.

They refueled the plane, gave him a terrifying "you-did-*not*-see-a-base" briefing, complete with threats about spending the rest of his life in prison if he told anyone what had happened, and then told him the distance and heading for Las Vegas. So, the pilot went on his way.

The next day, to the total disbelief of the air force, the same plane showed up again. Once again, the military police surrounded the plane, only this time there were two people on board. The same pilot jumped out and said, "do anything you want to me, but my wife is in the plane, and since I can't tell her where I was last night, I'm going to need you to."

We live in a world where faithfulness isn't often seen. A card company shows us the signs of our times well in this card: "I can't promise you forever, but I can promise you today." Here in the UK, we see a higher level of relationship breakdown now than we have in the past fifty years. For couples who were married in 1963, 23 percent had been divorced by the time they reached their twenty-fifth wedding anniversary. However, of couples who were married just over thirty years later, in 1996, 41 percent had divorced by their twenty-fifth wedding anniversary.[1]

Why is it that we find it so hard to trust politicians and those in power? Because so often what they have promised hasn't amounted to anything. Or they have said one thing and done another. Or what they promise changes so much on the winds of populism that we don't feel we have safe ground to stand on, let alone know what they stand for.

That is the depth of faithfulness that we often see displayed in our families, in our communities, in our governments—but all too sadly, often even in our churches.

We desperately need the Holy Spirit to grow faithfulness in our lives so that we might be able to live faithfully in a culture that far too often sees people as expendable.

THE IMAGE OF JESUS

Jesus modeled the fruit of faithfulness in various ways throughout his life and ministry, and his example teaches us how to remain faithful in our commitment to God and others.

Faithful to Who He Was: Temptation

One of the greatest challenges for Jesus came right at the very start of his ministry. Following his baptism, Jesus was led by the Spirit into the wilderness, during which time the devil tempted him.

Within the gospels there is a mirror between the ministry of Jesus and the history of Israel. Israel passes through the waters of the Red Sea and enters the wilderness where they will spend the next forty years.

Jesus passes through the waters of baptism and is led by the Spirit into the wilderness where he spends the next forty days.

Where Israel failed to live faithfully as God's people, Jesus remains faithful.

---

1. Data from Office of National Statistics.

FAITHFULNESS

In many ways this period of temptation is about remaining faithful to his identity as the son of his Father. When we look at the temptations in turn, we see that the first two come in the form of a question concerning Jesus' identity:

> "*If* you are the son of God . . ."[2]

The question that is often at the heart of temptation is one of faithfulness. Will we remain faithful to our covenant relationship with God, and to the identity he has given us, or will we take the path of less resistance?

For Jesus the path of faithfulness would lead to the cross. Yet where Israel failed in the desert, Jesus triumphed. He knew who he was. Just a few days beforehand the Spirit of God had descended on him and the Father had spoken clearly:

> "This is my Son, whom I love; with him I am well pleased."[3]

Faithfulness to God's Word

Notice as well during this time of temptation that Jesus remained faithful to God's word.

At the end of each temptation, when Jesus responds to the devil, he quotes scripture.

In response to the temptation to turn stones into bread, Jesus quotes Deuteronomy:

> " . . . man does not live on bread alone but on every word that comes from the mouth of the Lord."[4]

In response to the temptation to throw himself off the Temple, Jesus again quotes from Deuteronomy:

> "Do not put the Lord your God to the test."[5]

In response to the final temptation to bow down and worship Satan to receive the kingdoms of the world, Jesus quotes Deuteronomy for a third time:

2. Matt 4:3 and 6.
3. Matt 3:17.
4. Deut 8:3b.
5. Deut 6:16.

The Maker's Mark

"Worship the Lord your God and serve him only."[6]

What is interesting about the scriptures that Jesus quotes here from Deuteronomy is that they all come from passages that call the Israelites to live faithfully. They are speaking about how God has called his people out of slavery, given them a new identity and how they are to remain true to that identity, to be faithful to him even in a land of great temptation.

The Shema is one of the central prayers of the Jewish faith, and it would have prayed daily by Jesus, as it still is by Jews around the world today. It comes from this passage Jesus quotes from in Deuteronomy 6: "Hear, O Israel: The Lord our God, the Lord is one."[7] It continues to a well-known verse that Jesus quotes in Matthew 22: "Love the Lord your God with all your heart and with all your soul and with all your strength."[8]

What does biblical faithfulness look like? Loving the Lord your God with all your heart, soul and strength, even in the wilderness of temptation. Most of us are shrewd or discerning enough that if presented with a choice between right and wrong, or good and bad, we would choose the good and right path. What happens however when the bad is packaged up as good? That's the temptation. It mimics what is good, but it's not too long until you realize that you have been sold a lie.

That's why, as we saw with the fruit of goodness, we need to allow God to set the standard for what is good, and to stay close to him. That way we can not only discern good and bad, but also when we are being sold a poor imitation of the genuine article.

Jesus knew the scriptures. Many Jews learnt the scriptures from a very young age, memorizing great sections. In our western Christian culture, we struggle with a few memory verses in Sunday school.

How do we know that Jesus knew the scriptures? Because he either directly quotes from or refers to them around ninety times in the gospels.

In Matthew 21 Jesus tells the parable of the tenants, highlighting how the religious leaders of the nation have rejected both the messengers that God has sent, but also his own son. He ends the parable by quoting Psalm 118:22:

> "The stone the builders rejected
> has become the cornerstone."[9]

---

6. Deut 6:13.
7. Deut 6:4.
8. Deut 6:5.
9. Ps 118:22.

This is just one of several examples where Jesus quotes from the Psalms.[10] As we have already seen Jesus quotes from the Torah.[11] Jesus also draws on the prophetic tradition.[12]

The Hebrew Bible is broken into three sections; the Torah, the Prophets and The Writings, and across all four gospels, from the beginning of his ministry through to the end, we see Jesus quoting from every section of the scriptures.

Jesus was faithful to God's word because he knew God's word.

Like Father, Like Son

As we have already explored in previous chapters, the writer of Hebrews reminds us that Jesus is the exact representation of the Father. I have been blessed that I have inherited attributes of who I am that come from both my dad's. It's a subject that I explored in more depth in my book *Made to Belong*.

When those who knew my biological father (who died when I was three) recognize parts of him in me; mannerisms or character traits, it is always a lovely thing to hear. But equally I am like my dad, who married my Mum when I was seven years old. Parts of my personality and character are because of all that he has poured into my life over many years and I'm also proud to be his son. I hope and pray that there are good things in me that are passed down to my son, and that by God's grace he is saved from my faults and shortcomings.

Jesus and the Father are one and the same. They share the same essence and nature. This is part of the mystery of the Trinity, and while it's hard to get our heads around, it is an amazing comfort to us. Why? Because when many around the world are asking questions about what God is like, we don't need to get philosophical or deeply religious; we simply point them to Jesus. The same is true for each of us, as we wonder at times what God is really like; we look at Jesus. As Paul writes to the Colossians:

"We look at this Son and see the God who cannot be seen."[13]

---

10. See Ps 22:1 (Matt 27:46), Ps 110:1 (Matt 22:44) and Ps 82:6 (John 10:34).

11. For other examples see Exod 20:12–16 (Matt 19:18–19) and Lev 19:18 (Matt 22:39).

12. See Isa 61:1–2 (Luke 4:18–19), Isa 53:12 (Luke 22:37) and Jonah 1:17 (Matt 12:40).

13. Col 1:15, *Message*.

Jesus' character is full of faithfulness because the Father is full of faithfulness. We see examples of that throughout the Scriptures. Here are just a couple of examples.

> "I will proclaim the name of the Lord.
>   Oh, praise the greatness of our God!
> 4 He is the Rock, his works are perfect,
>   and all his ways are just.
> A faithful God who does no wrong,
>   upright and just is he."[14]

When we look at the word faithful in the Old Testament we come across the Hebrew word *Emet*. It can also be translated as *reliable, sure,* and *trustworthy*. The word *amen* that we say at the end of our prayers means *that's true*.

Jesus' character was reliable and stable. That's what his faithfulness looked like. Think about Jesus claim here in John 14:

> "I am the way and the truth and the life. No one comes to the Father except through me."[15]

Jesus doesn't just stand for truth or tell the truth. He *is* truth. Not only that, but he is *the* truth. In a world that offers many different versions of "truth," it is Jesus who is steady, reliable and trustworthy in the ever-changing landscape of our culture. That's why we refer to him as our Rock!

A God of Faithfulness

With God we see unwavering reliability in action. That reliability has been seen from generation to generation. Sometimes we avoid reading the genealogies that come at the start of both Matthew and Luke's gospel, because some of the names are hard to say and there isn't much action in the text. We can feel disconnected from the individuals mentioned because we don't always know very much about them. Yet the one thing we know about them is that they are woven into the tapestry of God's faithfulness and that can give us great confidence. If he has been faithful through all those generations, then why would he not be in ours? I think that is why God often speaks of himself as "the God of Abraham, Isaac and Jacob." I was faithful when I walked with Abraham. I was faithful when I walked with Issac. I

---

14. Deut 32:3–4.
15. John 14:6.

was faithful when I walked with Jacob. That's the God I am, and the God I will be. I was faithful before, and I will be faithful now. These genealogies, rather than being a long list of funny sounding names, are a journal of God's faithfulness throughout the generations.

Psalm 89 talks a lot about faithfulness. Let's just look at verses 1–8 for a moment:

> "I will sing of the LORD's great love forever;
> with my mouth I will make your faithfulness known through all generations.
> I will declare that your love stands firm forever, that you have established your faithfulness in heaven itself.
> You said, "I have made a covenant with my chosen one, I have sworn to David my servant,
> 'I will establish your line forever and make your throne firm through all generations.'"
> The heavens praise your wonders, LORD, your faithfulness too, in the assembly of the holy ones.
> For who in the skies above can compare with the LORD?
> Who is like the LORD among the heavenly beings?
> In the council of the holy ones God is greatly feared; he is more awesome than all who surround him.
> Who is like you, LORD God Almighty? You, LORD, are mighty, and your faithfulness surrounds you."[16]

What a song of praise! What is interesting is that this song of worship and praise was written, not in a time of celebration when everything was going well, but in a time of great difficultly, loneliness, suffering and pain. Even here, amid his pain the Psalmist cries out to God in praise for his faithfulness. Because God's faithfulness isn't measured by how good things are around you, or how well life is going. His faithfulness cannot be measured because it reaches up to the sky. God's faithfulness has been founded in heaven itself—the presence of God shows his faithfulness. And this is the God who has promised that he will never leave you or abandon you. It's easy to see the faithfulness of God when things are going according to the plan. It's easy to trust when things go as they should. It's easy to follow your satnav until it leads you down a road you don't recognize.

But what about when things don't go according to plan? What about times when, like the Psalmist, we suffer?

As the great hymn reminds us:

16. Ps 89:1–8.

The Maker's Mark

> "I cannot tell how silently he suffered,
> As with his peace he graced this place of tears,
> Or how his heart upon the Cross was broken,
> The crown of pain to three and thirty years.
>
> But this I know, he heals the broken-hearted,
> And stays our sin, and calms our lurking fear,
> And lifts the burden from the heavy laden,
> For yet the Savior, Savior of the world, is here."[17]

And this I know, that even in darkness, even in the silence; even in the places where you wonder where God is; even there, God is faithful. His faithfulness surrounds you.

What we see in Jesus is the face of the Faithful God, and for those of us who bear his mark, whose character is being shaped more and more like his, it is a fruit we need to bear.

THE FRUIT OF FAITHFULNESS

Living the fruit of faithfulness as a Christian is about embodying reliability, trust, and steadfast devotion to God and others in every aspect of life. When Paul writes to the Romans he says this:

> "So here's what I want you to do, God helping you: Take your everyday, ordinary life—your sleeping, eating, going-to-work, and walking-around life—and place it before God as an offering. Embracing what God does for you is the best thing you can do for him.
> Don't become so well-adjusted to your culture that you fit into it without even thinking. Instead, fix your attention on God. You'll be changed from the inside out. Readily recognize what he wants from you and quickly respond to it. Unlike the culture around you, always dragging you down to its level of immaturity, God brings the best out of you, develops well-formed maturity in you."[18]

One of the words that is very much part of the culture we live in today is *trend*. It's a funny concept to pin down but it is when a certain behavior, style, idea, or movement becomes popular and gains momentum in society

---

17. W. Y. Fullerton, "I Cannot Tell" (1920).
18. Rom 12:1–2, *Message*.

for a period. We see this in fashion, technology, social media and culture more generally.

Here is the thing to bear in mind with trends though; they come and go. That might seem obvious, but people move from one trend to another all the time simply because it is popular and then wonder why their lives feel unstable.

Trends in and of themselves aren't bad, but we should always be wise in discerning why we are following that trend (is it me following the crowd) and whether the trend is leading us towards or away from God. Rather than being carried along by the crowd from one trend to the other, when we focus on the one who does not change, we can live faithfully.

Let's explore some of the key ways we can cultivate the fruit of faithfulness in our everyday, ordinary lives as we seek to grow in Jesus shaped character.

Stay Rooted in Scripture

One of the challenges that we have as Christians in remaining faithful to God is that the values of the world we live in shift all the time. What was considered wrong yesterday may be celebrated today. Despite this, God's Word doesn't change. The prophet Isaiah reminds us:

> "The grass withers and the flowers fall, but the word of our God endures for ever."[19]

An important part of knowing how to live faithfully is knowing God's heart. The scriptures are the only reliable information we have about God, and yet there are times when we treat them so casually. But when the Holy Spirit breathes life into his word, those words can come alive and be life for us as we read them.

As a family we try to root ourselves in reading the scriptures together daily, and to prioritize that time. We ask questions, we share what has struck us from the passage, and we see how it can apply to our lives. What are your patterns for staying rooted in scripture?

As I said at the start of this chapter, Jesus was rooted in the scriptures. He knew them and lived them out consistently. If we want to have character that is shaped like Jesus, then just like Jesus we need to spend time regularly

---

19. Isa 40:8.

reading, meditating on, and applying the scriptures to our lives. That keeps us anchored in truth rather than opinions.

Last year as a church we read through the Bible in a year, and one of the main reasons for doing that was that we would know God's word. Each of us have our favorite passages that are a comfort and a strength to us. We can easily lay our hands on passages that are an encouragement. But the beauty of reading God's word all the way through is that you come across passages that will challenge and disturb you too. You will come across passages that cause you to ask questions, and to live with the tensions within scripture.

One of the reasons why people have a crisis of faith when hard times come, is that they have used the Bible as a motivational self-help book, and never been disturbed by it, or asked questions because of it. They haven't allowed it to shape and transform them. When life becomes disturbing or full of questions, they don't know how to live faithfully. That is hard, as anyone who has been in those moments can testify to, but living faithfully *is* hard at times.

When we know his word, then it will start to guide the decisions that we make and the paths that we take in life's journey. Some Bibles will have a "life guide" at the front, where you can search for passages depending on what you are going through in life at that moment in time. They are a useful tool in helping to apply scripture to your life, and in doing so learning how to live faithfully to who he has called you to be.

Remain in Jesus

Faithfulness isn't just about *doing Christian things*; it's about *knowing Christ personally*. Through prayer, worship, confession, and daily dependence, we are transformed more into the image of Jesus, and more able to live faithfully for him in the areas he has placed us in.

Jesus reminds his disciples:

> "Remain in me, as I also remain in you. No branch can bear fruit by itself; it must remain in the vine. Neither can you bear fruit unless you remain in me.
> "I am the vine; you are the branches. If you remain in me and I in you, you will bear much fruit; apart from me you can do nothing."[20]

20. John 15:4–5.

Jesus' call to *remain in me* is an invitation into faithful intimacy with him. Faithfulness, as a fruit, is cultivated as we remain in him daily: trusting, obeying, loving, and persevering.

It incorporates all that I have mentioned about the scriptures, but also includes worship, prayer and devotion. It is the placing of our whole lives before Jesus as an offering.

Jesus is calling for a faithful, enduring relationship with him. This isn't just putting a tick in a box, praying a believer's prayer one-time kind of commitment; it implies spiritual constancy, loyalty, and perseverance, even when circumstances test our faith.

What we find is that the more we seek to faithfully remain in Jesus, the more he produces it within us. Faithfulness is the fruit of the Spirit; it grows and flourishes in our lives because of living in the Spirit. In that sense faithfulness is both a requirement *and* a result of remaining in Jesus.

One of the reasons why prayer is part of what we call spiritual *disciplines* is because it takes exactly that, discipline, to really grow in our prayer lives. When it comes to remaining in Jesus, to cultivating an intimate relationship with him, it takes discipline. There are so many distractions in life that fight for our time and attention, and hopefully many of them are good. However, what could be greater than spending time in the presence of Jesus, to be found in him, to be known as *his*: his beloved. Wouldn't spending time with him help you and inspire you to live more faithfully for him?

Be Part of a Strong Community

Faithful Christians don't walk alone. The early church survived under hostile Roman culture because they met regularly, prayed together, encouraged each other, and bore each other's burdens. You need community to grow in faithfulness. The writer of Hebrews encourages us:

> "And let us consider how we may spur one another on toward love and good deeds, not giving up meeting together, as some are in the habit of doing, but encouraging one another—and all the more as you see the Day approaching."[21]

Church can be a community where faithfulness flourishes. I hope that many of you reading this have had times in church where it has spurred you on towards a deeper life of faithfulness to Jesus. Not just in the worship and

---

21. Heb 10:24–25.

teaching, the liturgy and prayers; but through the people. The community of gathered believers who seek a common and unique faithfulness to Jesus and his way of living. If we are in the habit of giving up meeting together, it won't be all that long before we fall into the habit of giving up. Giving up prayer, giving up worship, giving up reading the scriptures, giving up on faithfulness to Jesus.

I've been part of a church community since I was born and pastored in them for almost half my life. There are two things I have found that really make a community thrive as a place where faithfulness can flourish: humility and vulnerability.

Other people within your community can only spur you on if you are willing to learn from them, and you are only willing to learn if you don't think you know everything. When people within the church take a posture of humility, not only are they able to live like Jesus, but we also open ourselves up to the guidance and encouragement of those who walk the road with us.

When it comes to church leaders, we need to reprioritize humility as key to community leadership. So many church leaders fall into the trap of trying to be successful. What's wrong with being successful you might ask? Well in and of itself nothing really, but it is the means that we use to get to it that often causes the problem. We think that *success* is like this other church over here that has five times the number of people going to it. They have a great social media presence and slick online engagement. When we hold other churches up as successful, and we prioritize success then we start to think that we need to be like them.

If you look at the early churches, the ones that Paul wrote to many times, would you have called them successful? Or the seven churches in Revelation that the Lord tells John to write to? These churches were riddled with infighting and peppered with doctrinal squabbling. They didn't have social media or a record-label worthy worship team. Based on many of our modern-day measures of success they didn't make the cut.

But they were faithful.

What if God is calling us to be the same, not successful, but faithful. Humility is key to that.

Vulnerability is key because unless I am willing to share with others then there isn't a space for them to share with me. We must be open to sharing our needs as well as our advice and our weaknesses as well as our strengths. Our vulnerability helps us to identify with others and to share each other's burdens. Faithfulness in the context of community cannot thrive unless it grows in the rich soil of humility and vulnerability.

Embrace a Lifestyle of Integrity

If we want to live faithfully then we need to embrace a lifestyle of integrity, of wholeness of character. We need to be honest and reliable. One of the ways we can translate the word for faithfulness conveys truthfulness. We live honestly. That means far more than simply not telling lies but making choices that are compatible with the character of Jesus and the character that he is seeking to grow within us. It's more than the absence of bad things, but it is living consistently in all we do.

It's lived out in the small things as well as the big things. Integrity is not just about grand gestures but about being faithful in the unseen and the everyday. As Jesus taught us:

> "Whoever can be trusted with very little can also be trusted with much."[22]

Integrity is consistency in doing what's right, even when it's not seen, noticed or rewarded.

It also comes in fearing God and not people. I heard a story a long time ago about a pastor who visited another pastor in prison. The pastor in the story wasn't named, and neither was the reason for his imprisonment. The visiting pastor talked with him for a while, and then, curious after all that he had heard, asked the question "when did you stop loving Jesus?"

The former pastor replied, surprised at the question, "That was never the problem, I never stopped loving Jesus, the problem was that I stopped *fearing God.*"

We don't talk about fearing God enough.

What can lure us into fearing people more than God is the rise of populism in our society. Make no mistake, it has always been there. It is the politics of shortcuts and the breeding ground of lazy morality. It highlights tribalism over care for the marginalized and identity based on group narratives rather than being rooted in Jesus. We have politicians all around the world who will develop an ideology rooted in populism to win votes, whether they believe in their own message or not. Albert Einstein once famously said:

22. Luke 16:10.

"What is right is not always popular, and what is popular is not always right."

The values of our culture shift, even what is perceived to be *truth* shifts, blown by the winds of populism. Yet Jesus said:

"My kingdom is not of this world."[23]

In the face a populist culture the gospel calls us to a higher loyalty, to Jesus and his faithful way of peace, mercy, and justice.

At the beginning of the chapter, we reflected together on how Jesus was faithful during temptation. The third and final temptation the devil tried involved Jesus bowing down before him to claim all the kingdoms of the world. These kingdoms, indeed, all creation, were Jesus' to begin with. To win them back though, he had to go to the cross. What the devil presents Jesus with here is a shortcut. You can have the glory you're due, but you don't have to go through all the pain and anguish of the cross. Now that's tempting, right? Pastor David Hansen reflects on this:

> "We pimp shortcuts. Everybody wants them. People will pay good money for them. We love cheap love and hate the costly cross. By giving people shortcuts, we are cheating them out of life in Christ, and it destroys us."[24]

When we fear people more than we fear God we are tempted to take shortcuts. Shortcuts are not compatible with consistent living. Shortcuts do not foster integrity. Shortcuts do not grow faithfulness. Jesus lived with integrity, in the small things and the big, in the moments of praise and the moments of temptation. He honored God above all others and walked in faithfulness with him.

TENDING THE SOIL

So, what are some of the weeds that can stifle the growth of the fruit of faithfulness in our lives?

---

23. John 18:36.
24. Hansen, *Art of Pastoring*, 77.

Lack of a Strong Relationship with Jesus

This might sound obvious, but it can be easily neglected. Most of us have had times when spiritually we have been going through the motions. We've showed up to church, sung the songs, prayed the prayers, chatted with others, but if we are honest, our hearts haven't been in it. There are times when we neglect prayer, Bible study, and fellowship with God, and in those times our faithfulness weakens.

Where I live in the Southwest of the UK, we have just had a bit of a heatwave. Don't get too excited for me, it's a heatwave by UK standards, but what it has meant is that I have had to make sure that I water the plants in the garden more often. One plant I need to pay attention to is my tomato plant. My son and I have been involved in a bit of a tomato race, planting fallen tomatoes from last year's plants and seeing who's will grow and produce fruit first. I thought he had been watering both our plants when he had been watering the garden (as I had been), but it turns out he was paying particular attention to his plant and NO attention to mine. You can tell, because my plant is withered and lifeless, with no fruit. Leos are healthy, with little tomatoes starting to grow.

There is a lesson there for us as we seek to live with the fruit of faithfulness in our characters.

Just like a plant needs water, our faithfulness needs to be nurtured through a strong relationship with Jesus. We need his living water to grow healthy, strong and consistently. Without it, we wither and fail to produce anything, especially in the heatwaves of life.

Self-Reliance Rather than Dependence on God

Another danger for us here is when we try to do everything in our own strength rather than relying on God. Think about what Jesus said when speaking of himself as the vine:

"Apart from me you can do *nothing*."

The Greek is far more emphatic: *not one thing!*

The challenge for us here is that we are often brought up in a culture that values independence. We teach our children to be self-sufficient, and we praise those who are financially independent. Society looks down on people with benefits because we feel that people *should* be able to get by on their own, and that this is a measure of their success.

If we are not careful the same thing can creep into our spirituality as well. We think that we can do it alone, that somehow, we have acquired enough spiritual knowledge to be able to live the Christian life our way. My strength will get me so far, but when it's run out I get into trouble. My strength, energy, goodness, spirituality is finite. When I rely on my own strength, I can become weary and frustrated. Solomon was right in his teaching:

> "Trust in the Lord with all your heart
> and *lean not on your own understanding*;
> in all your ways submit to him,
> and he will make your paths straight."[25]

Faithfulness grows when we trust in God's strength, not just our own abilities.

Distracted

We are saturated with stuff, yet we are hungry for more. We comfort-eat from materialism, yet we are hungrier than ever. As John Piper wrote:

> "The greatest enemy of hunger for God is not poison but apple pie. It is not the banquet of the wicked that dulls our appetite for heaven, but endless nibbling at the table of the world."[26]

What does that *nibble* look like for you? The relentless pursuit of more? Getting caught in the trap of a bigger house or a better car, a higher paid job? Is it spending time together with the *right people* or being seen at the best social events? As the hymn writer says, reflecting on the challenges of 1960's Britian, we often have:

> ". . . spirits oppressed by pleasure, wealth and care."[27]

The love of material things, pursuit of success, entertainment, and social pressures can shift our focus away from God. When Jesus tells the parable of the Sower, he warns what the effects these things can have on us:

---

25. Prov 3:5–6, Emphasis my own.
26. Piper, *Hunger for God*, 14.
27. Dudley Smith, *Lord for the Years*.

> "But the worries of this life, the deceitfulness of wealth and the desires for other things come in and choke the word, making it unfruitful."[28]

They choke the life from us, and they stop us from being fruitful. If we are constantly distracted by these things, hunger after these things, then we will struggle to develop the fruit of faithfulness in our lives.

What might be distracting you? Is it the pursuit of more? Is it the constant scrolling of social media? God is ready to prune away those thorns which choke the fruitfulness from you, so that you can life faithfully.

Unhealed Wounds

Each of us experiences wounds. It is often the wounds from others that cause the most pain. The most painful moments of rejection come from those whose role it was to embrace you. The most hurt can come from those who were called to protect you. There are many of you reading this today who know the pain of putting your heart out there, and rather than someone catching it, they stamped on it.

I don't want in any way to downplay those wounds and simply say that we need to get over them. That isn't always possible. Forgiveness is not necessarily about a reunion; it is about release. Forgiveness when it's painful, messy and unresolved, is for *your* freedom, not for *their* right to continued access to you. It is possible to forgive, release and move on, without ever explaining yourself or reopening old wounds. However, there can be dangers to living with unhealed wounds when it comes to living faithfully.

Holding grudges against others can harden our hearts and make it difficult to remain faithful to God's command to love and forgive. Paul writes:

> "Get rid of all bitterness, rage and anger, brawling and slander, along with every form of malice. Be kind and compassionate to one another, forgiving each other, just as in Christ God forgave you."[29]

Several years ago, I came across a modern-day proverb which has always stuck with me:

> "If you don't heal what hurt you, you'll bleed on people who didn't cut you."[30]

---

28. Mark 4:19.
29. Eph 4:31–32.
30. Unattributed.

The Maker's Mark

Think of those times that you have been hurt by someone, and in that hurt, lashed out at another person who was totally unresponsible for your hurt? A partner, a child, a colleague? They were in the wrong place at the wrong time, and they got bled on.

Some wounds are deep, and they take years to heal. As we bring those wounds to God, sometimes seventy-seven times, he can bring healing and even teach us to find things to be thankful for, which is the antidote to the bitterness that often can accompany our wounds. A heart weighed down by bitterness struggles to grow in faithfulness.

Bring your wounds to God, who is not only uniquely able to hold you in that place of pain but is able to give you the strength through the tender power of his Spirit to love the unlovable like he does and live faithfully in that place too.

Faithfulness is the Maker's mark.

QUESTIONS FOR REFLECTION

1. How would you define faithfulness?
2. What are the ways you struggle to stay faithful during times of temptation?
3. What are your Bible reading patterns? How would you like to grow in faithfulness in this area of your life?
4. In the ever-changing landscape of our culture, how can believing that Jesus is *the* way help us to live faithfully?
5. How are you actively seeking to *remain* in Jesus?
6. Would you describe yourself as humble and vulnerable? How would your community be a place of greater faithfulness if you modeled these qualities?
7. Considering our discussion on populism, how would you answer the question "are my views shaped more by my faith in Christ or by political identity?"
8. In what ways would you like your relationship with Jesus to be deeper?
9. What are the things in your life now that distract you from living faithfully? How might you lay these things down?
10. How can bitterness stop us living faithfully?

10

Gentleness

WE EACH HAVE OUR own ideas about the word gentleness and what it means. And if most of us are honest it doesn't seem like the most appealing fruit. When we think of the other fruits, about love, and peace and joy, they seem appealing. We want those in our lives, but gentleness?

One of the issues we have with gentleness is the way in which the word has been given to us over the years. The King James Version of the Bible has translated this word as "meekness." Who wants to be meek? It is a word that has fallen out of popular use in modern times. What image does that conjure up? Quiet, gentle, easily imposed on.

When we think about those characteristics many people say, "I'm not sure I really want to be like that."

When we look at the Greek word before it was translated, looking at the different ways it was used, then we get a different picture altogether.

The Greeks used this word to describe strong animals that were brought under control.

Aristotle spoke of the "gentle" elephant; and Plato described a mighty and strong beast which could be tamed and fed by a person who learned how to handle it.

The well-known theologian William Barclay says the best illustration is the watchdog "who is bravely hostile to strangers and gently friendly with familiars whom he knows and loves."

THE IMAGE OF JESUS

As we come to look at how Jesus embodies this fruit, there is something we need to understand when we talk about gentleness:

Gentleness is not weakness.

It might surprise you to know that there are only two individuals that the Bible describes by using the word *gentle*: Jesus and Moses.

You wouldn't describe either of these as weak, or "easy imposed on." You wouldn't find either cowering in the corner.

Their gentleness was not weakness; it was a heart surrendered to God, a teachable spirit, a gentle strength.

Let me give you a definition of gentleness: Gentleness is power under control. Or more importantly, it is power under God's control.

The animal that has been tamed, to use the analogy of the ancient Greeks, allows the master to control them. The same then is true of gentleness. That the strength and the power that we have is one that is controlled by God. It is placing our power under the control of God.

There is a hymn that begins with the line "Little Jesus meek and mild."

Gentleness is that attitude of spirit to accept God's dealings with us as good and not dispute or resist. That's quite at odds with the traditional understanding of meekness.

Think about Jesus clearing the tables of the money changers in Matthew 21.

Little Jesus, meek and mild ... really? Jesus got angry. He wasn't meek in that traditional sense of the word. He wasn't passive. But he was gentle in the sense that his anger, his power, was under control and channeled in the right direction.

Jesus lived out the fruit of the Spirit of gentleness in profound and consistent ways throughout his life and ministry. His gentleness was always directed by love and humility. Let's look at some of the ways Jesus embodied this fruit.

Embracing the Overlooked

Jesus welcomed the weak and the vulnerable, as well as giving time and value to those who society placed little value on.

Think about how Jesus engaged with women. There is a great example of Jesus speaking with the woman at the well in Samaria. When we read the

GENTLENESS

conversation in John 4 we can see it is one full of gentleness. Jesus is aware of the situation and the power dynamic here. She is a woman, alone with a man, which puts her in a vulnerable situation. He is a Jew, and she is a Samaritan, which adds to the tension.

She is drawing water from the well around noon, which is the hottest part of the day and far from the ideal time for this task. Why was she not drawing water with the other women? Perhaps it was because her personal situation, which is complicated to say the least, alienated her from her community.

Despite all the tension in the background of this encounter, Jesus engages with the woman in a gentle way. His questions, his teaching and his engagement with her are non-threatening. Even when he makes it clear that he is aware of her complicated personal life, there is very much a tone of gentleness:

> "Jesus said to her, 'You are right when you say you have no husband. The fact is, you have had five husbands, and the man you now have is not your husband. What you have just said is quite true.'"[1]

Women were often badly treated in Jesus' culture, as they sadly still are at times today, by men who feel they need to exert their power over them. Jesus' manner is one that puts the woman at ease and draws her into this encounter.

When he hears of her situation, there is no judgement or condemnation. The tone of the conversation does not change. Jesus remains gentle.

As well as his engagement with women, the way that Jesus encountered children gives us a good picture of his gentleness too.

> "Let the little children come to me, and do not hinder them, for the kingdom of heaven belongs to such as these."[2]
>
> Even though children were considered socially insignificant in Jesus' time, he treated them with gentleness and value. He not only welcomed them, but he challenged us to become like them in our simple and trusting faith.

Children have often been treated badly by society. Think of the phrase "children should be seen and not heard," and think about the message that

---

1. John 4:17–18.
2. Matt 19:14.

this communicates about the value and worth of children? Is that gentleness? Is that welcome? I read recently:

> "We remain faithful to the way of Jesus, who took a child into his arms and saw her for the unique person she was, when we offer radical hospitality to children for who they are, regardless of their race, interests, socioeconomic background, gender and so on."[3]

There are many others whom Jesus welcomed, but in doing so he showed a heart that stood in opposition to the hardness of his culture, gently yet purposefully drawing others in.

Invitation to Rest

It is important to understand that *we* not only perceive Jesus as gentle, but that Jesus called *himself* gentle:

> "Come to me, all you who are weary and burdened, and I will give you rest. Take my yoke upon you and learn from me, for I am *gentle* and humble in heart, and you will find rest for your souls."[4]

This is one of the clearest self-descriptions of his gentle nature. Why does that matter? Because when you are weary and weak, you need someone who is going to be gentle with you. You need someone who is going to meet you in a place of gentleness and rest. In a fast-paced world, a world of noise and speed, often people find themselves burned out and struggling to cope with the demands of life. Stop the world, I want to get off, is the cry of many weary hearts.

How does Jesus meet us in those moments? With gentleness.

This verse is the only place in the Gospels where Jesus explicitly describes his own heart, and so it's especially significant that he chooses *gentle* and *lowly*. His call to rest is not just a statement of intent; it's a revelation of who he is. He doesn't just speak or act gently. He is gentle.

There are two things which stand out about his gentleness here.

Firstly, Jesus calls out specifically to those who are burdened and exhausted. He doesn't expect people to meet him with strength or perfection but rather he meets them in their weakness.

---

3. Csinos and Beckwith, *Children's Ministry in the Way of Jesus*, 14.
4. Matt 11:28–29.

Gentleness

One of the most well received books I have written is my book *Infused with Life*, which explores God's gift of rest in a world of busyness. This book wasn't well received because it was especially well written, but because I think most of us know all too well those moments of exhaustion, when you are at the end of yourself and you know what you need is someone to meet you in that place and offer you the one thing that is hard to come by: genuine rest. When Jesus meets us in that place, calling out to us, that's gentleness. He stoops to lift us up rather than standing back in judgment. As Isaiah says:

> "A bruised reed he will not break,
> and a smoldering wick he will not snuff out."[5]

Secondly, what Jesus offers highlights his gentleness. He does not offer another burden, but rest. That stands in contrast with the religious leaders of Jesus' day as we see later in Matthew's gospel:

> "Then Jesus said to the crowds and to his disciples: 'The teachers of the law and the Pharisees sit in Moses' seat. So, you must be careful to do everything they tell you. But do not do what they do, for they do not practice what they preach. They tie up heavy, cumbersome loads and put them on other people's shoulders, but they themselves are not willing to lift a finger to move them.'"[6]

Unlike the religious leaders of the day who loaded people with rules and obligations Jesus offers rest, both spiritual, physical and emotional. Often people see and experience religion as putting burden after burden on them, an endless set of rules that they can never measure up to. That adds to a sense of burnout because there is no safe ground on which to stand and catch your breath. To the tired, worn-out and weary, another regulation or burden is hardly going to instill in them a sense of life.

Jesus doesn't coerce or shame people into following but invites them to come and experience his gentleness in the form of rest. His approach reflects the gentleness of a shepherd, not the pressure of a demanding taskmaster.

---

5. Isa 42:3.
6. Matt 23:1–4.

The Maker's Mark

Gentleness that Mends

There were lots of people who Jesus healed, but his gentleness is also shown in the way that he healed. Let me give you two examples.

Firstly, there is the account of Jesus healing the man with leprosy at the beginning of Mark's gospel:

> "A man with leprosy came to him and begged him on his knees, 'If you are willing, you can make me clean.'
> Jesus was filled with compassion. He reached out his hand and touched the man. 'I am willing,' he said. 'Be clean!' Immediately the leprosy left him and he was cleansed."[7]

I don't think we can underestimate the power of the words *he reached out his hand and touched the man*.

People with leprosy were social and religious outcasts, rejected by their family, friends and the community at large. According to the law they were considered spiritually unclean, which meant they had to live outside of the community. Whenever they came near people, they had to shout the words *unclean* as a warning to others not to come near.[8]

Many people suffering with this condition would not have been touched by another person, or shown gentleness in any way, potentially for years. Can you imagine that? To have not been touched, embraced, shown tenderness or gentleness, for *years*! To have someone break through that level of isolation and exclusion must be world shattering.

The second example is the healing of the woman healed of bleeding, which we can find in Mark 5. Having suffered with bleeding for twelve years, in desperation she reaches out to Jesus through the crowd and touches the hem of his robe. She is instantly healed. Jesus feels the power leave him and asks who has touched him. Mark gives us an account of what happens next:

> "Then the woman, knowing what had happened to her, came and fell at his feet and, trembling with fear, told him the whole truth. He said to her, 'Daughter, your faith has healed you. Go in peace and be freed from your suffering.'"[9]

The woman comes in fear, but Jesus meets her with gentleness. He calls her daughter. How restoring must that have been for a person who

---

7. Mark 1:40–42.
8. Lev 13:45–46.
9. Mark 5:32–34.

would have been rejected by her family due to the nature of her illness. Society cast her out, but the gentleness of Jesus not only mends her body but restores her into family.

Jesus bore the fruit of gentleness.

THE FRUIT OF GENTLENESS

In the age we live in, gentleness isn't always seen as the most appealing fruit. Deeper than that though, if we are honest, is the reality that gentleness is a fruit that doesn't come naturally to us either. In a world where we see strength and power used without restraint, we really need the Spirit to work with us and within us to develop this fruit in our lives.

I have said several times throughout this book that it is the Spirit of God who grows this fruit in us. That's why it's called the fruit of the Spirit. But there are things that we can do to cultivate that fruit, to aid its growth, to work in partnership with the Holy Spirit in seeing that fruit grow into maturity. The same is true when it comes to the fruit of gentleness.

Obedient to God

Paul put it like this:

> "In your relationships with one another, have the same mind-set as Christ Jesus:
> Who, being in very nature God,
>   did not consider equality with God something to be used to his own advantage;
> rather, he made himself nothing
>   by taking the very nature of a servant,
>   being made in human likeness.
> And being found in appearance as a man,
>   he humbled himself
>   by becoming obedient to death—
>   even death on a cross!"[10]

If gentleness is power under control, or rather, under God's control, then we must begin by being obedient to the will and leading of God. We must learn to submit, which isn't a word that we are all that comfortable with. If we are going to be gentle, we must relinquish our power to God. Why? If we

10. Phil 2:5–8.

cannot be submissive or obedient to the will of God, we will have trouble being gentle, because we will be operating under our own control. We will be relying on our own strength, power, and agenda.

We think about submitting to the will of God as an authoritarian action. That's not the image often used in scripture. Think about David's well-loved Psalm:

> "You have bedded me down in lush meadows,
>   you find me quiet pools to drink from.
> True to your word,
>   you let me catch my breath
>   and send me in the right direction."[11]

The shepherd will purposefully lead the sheep, but it is always with the best interest of the sheep in mind. The shepherd may require the sheep to move, to journey even through the darkest valleys, but it is to lead the sheep to the quiet pools and the lush meadows. It is in submitting to the will and the leading of the shepherd that the sheep experiences the gentleness of life.

If we want to be gentle, then we need to learn to lay ourselves down and to be led by the Spirit. Then we can be open to those he leads us to. Then we will start to see those we come across, not simply as random encounters, but as those whom he has led us to. Then we will be a place where gentleness can flow.

Teachable Spirits

If we think we know it all already, we will never grow, and if we cannot grow, we will not be able to be the gentle person God invites us to be.

Whether you are eighteen or eighty, life is a journey of learning. Let me encourage you to keep growing. Keep opening yourself up to God's Spirit cultivating your life.

James writes:

> "Therefore lay aside all filthiness and overflow of wickedness, and receive with gentleness the implanted word, which is able to save your souls."[12]

Or as the Message beautifully puts it:

---

11. Ps 23:2–3, *Message*.
12. Jas 1:21, *New King James Version*.

"Let our gardener, God, landscape you with the Word, making a salvation-garden of your life."[13]

We must be willing to learn and grow. One of the challenges within our churches is that there are too many of us who do not have teachable spirits. There is a big difference between thinking we are right and possessing the truth.

Having a teachable spirit is part of the way we can understand what God's will is because we open ourselves up to knowing what is on God's heart, to learn his mind, and to be willing to respond.

A teachable spirit is part of being obedient to the will of God. It is God's will for us to grow, to flourish and to thrive. Are we willing to do that? Are we willing to grow in gentleness?

Gentleness Towards Others

Empathy is so important. The ability to put yourself in the place of another person. To try and understand what it is like to be where they are. To put ourselves in their shoes.

Ephesians 4:1–2 says:

> "I, the prisoner of the Lord, implore you to walk in a manner worthy of the calling with which you have been called, with all humility and gentleness, with patience, showing tolerance for one another in love."

Are you tolerant of others? Are you considerate of others? Do you try to place yourself in the shoes of others? Can you empathize with others?

It's all part of what it means to cultivate the fruit of gentleness in your life.

Empathy acknowledges the other person's point of view. It can give validation to their feelings while not necessarily agreeing with them. When we do this we open a space where we can communicate, where we can step outside of ourselves and see the value and worth in another.

Gentleness doesn't force the issue but creates a space in which the other person is seen and heard.

---

13. Jas 1:21, *Message*.

A Calm Presence in a Stormy World

If we are honest, most of us are affected far more by the world around us than we would like. That is especially true when it comes to being calm. Some of this links back to what we explored in the fruit of patience, but it's hard to underplay just how important calmness is to gentleness. If gentleness is the fruit, then calmness is the branch that bears it.

How do I know I need to be calmer? I have a fragrance candle in my study with a scent called "calm." And it really does what it says on the tin.

The world around us makes it hard to feel calm. We are bombarded by imagery that ramps up our stress levels. There are times when I sit and watch the news, and I'm stressed by all the things I see happening around the world, even though for all of them there is nothing I can personally do to change them. Demands at work, family health issues, rising costs, uncertain global situations, all of them cause me to worry. That worry then affects my presence in the world and how that shapes those around me.

What I want is to be calm. What I find is that much like James Bond's Martini, I'm shaken not stirred. Not stirred by the gentle rest of the Spirit, or by my desire to be a good husband or father but shaken by the constant assault of information and demand that most of us know now as "normal life."

Mark Sayers wrote a great book called *A Non-Anxious Presence*, where he reminds us of this:

> " . . . despite how much we try and rationally think through our issues, we will find ourselves enveloped within a system of chronic anxiety."[14]

Does that ring any bells? If it does, then you will know all too well how hard it is to be gentle in this culture. What we need is not better coping mechanisms alone, although there is certainly a place for them, but we need the storm to be calmed.

There are two images that spring to mind.

The first is when Jesus calms the wind and the waves when the storm rages across the sea of Galilee in Mark 4. The disciples are terrified and afraid that they're going to drown. They call out to Jesus, and he calms the storm. Maybe that's how you feel, powerless and terrified at the winds and the waves that rage around you? Call out to Jesus because he has the power to calm the storm.

The second image comes right at the start of the Bible, in Genesis 1:

14. Sayers, *Non-Anxious Presence*, 97.

"Now the earth was formless and empty, darkness was over the surface of the deep, and the Spirit of God was hovering over the waters."[15]

The waters of chaos before the creation might be where you feel you are now. Nothing especially easy to pinpoint, but a sense of tumultuous foreboding within you. A rising sense of overwhelm. As hard as this place might seem, here there is the potential for creation. The Spirit of God is here, hovering over the waters. Like a mother bird flutters her wings over her eggs to encourage her chicks to hatch, the Spirit of God is hovering over you, drawing you closer to that new birth. And that comes, not so much with a big bang, but with a simple voice. A gentle voice, bringing with it light and creative life.

What I often do though is think of the wind and the waves as things around me that are affecting me. Stresses and strains, worries and wants. What if I am the sea? What if it is me that needs to be calmed. What if the voice of Jesus is not speaking to the issues that bombard me, but to *me* personally . . . be still. That it is not my life that becomes calm, but *I* become calm.

When I am calm, I can be gentle. When I am calm, I can see and value others. When I am calm, I can submit to the direction and leading of God. Perhaps then my gentleness will be a harbor of calm in the story seas for others.

The Golden Rule

The concept of not harming others is common across religions and cultures.

A couple of decades before the time of Jesus, there were two prominent Rabbis, Hillel and Shammai. There is a popular story about a gentile who is visiting Israel, and goes first to Rabbi Shammai and says, "if you can tell me the whole Torah while I am standing on one leg, then I will convert." In one version of the story Shamai gets cross and chases the man away with a stick. So, the man goes next to Rabbi Hillel and asks him the same question. Hillel responds: "What is hateful to you, do not do to your neighbor; that is the whole Torah; the rest is commentary."[16]

---

15. Gen 1:2.
16. Talmud Bavli, tractate Shabbat 31a.

The Maker's Mark

I recently came across someone breaking this teaching down into three rules. The wooden rule, the silver rule and the golden rule.

The wooden rule can be summarized as *do to others what they do to you*. This is the way of the world. It is reactionary and retaliatory in both positive and negative ways. In a positive way it's "you scratch my back, I'll scratch yours," or it's buying someone a present because they bought you one. In a negative way it's "tit for tat," or if you're unkind to me then I'll do the same to you. In the evolution of human social development, it is the lowest level, but it is sadly the level that a lot of people get stuck in. If you aren't sure about that, just look at the comment section on any contentious social media post.

It's easy to get sucked into this way of thinking in both the positive and negative sense, but it's certainly not the gentle way of Jesus.

Then you have the silver rule, which says *don't do to others what you wouldn't want done to you*. This is a great rule to live by, and it is one that predates Jesus' teachings. We have already seen it in the Rabbinic teachings of the late first century BC, but it was also an important school of thought in East Asia. Buddhism highlights the importance of the silver rule: "Hurt not others in ways that you yourself would find hurtful."[17]

The world would certainly be a better place, and our relationships would be much richer if we followed the silver rule, but the challenge with it is that it's framed very much in the negative.

If all relational teaching in the Bible can be condensed into "love you neighbor as you love yourself," then the golden rule is how we do that:

"Do to others as you would have them do to you."[18]

It is about gentleness in action.

This doesn't just require us to place ourselves in the shoes of others, but far more intimately, to place others in our shoes and then treat them as we would want to be treated. It is the projection of self-protection onto others, then enveloping of others into our gentle self-care. It is all the best and the good I want for myself, offered with all the gentleness I desire, but to those around me.

What you desire for yourself, desire it for others. Think of how you would like to be treated and then seize the initiative and treat others like that.

17. Udanavarga 5:18.
18. Luke 6:31.

Gentleness

Gentleness is not weakness, but power under control. When we are motivated by the golden rule, we can express ourselves gently. We can treat others with dignity, tenderness and respect.

Watch Your Tone

Gentleness isn't just about *what* we do, but about *how* we do it. That's tone. Following on from thinking about the golden rule, think about this situation. If you found yourself in a place where you needed to be corrected or helped, how would you want the other person to do that? I'd imagine that a key part of that would be around "tone." You'd want them to be kind, to be constructive, and to be gentle.

Think about a situation where someone has rubbed you up the wrong way. They have said something that has upset you. I would imagine that a lot of that has to do with tone.

When I speak to Bex and Leo in a way that falls short of what I want and they deserve, most of the time that has to do with tone. It's hard to receive the message of love and gentleness when it is delivered with a sledgehammer, sarcasm, impatience, irritability or haughtiness.

Much like we have already seen with loving our neighbor as we love ourselves, how we treat others has an awful lot to do with how we treat ourselves. If we want to be gentle with others, then we need to know how to be gentle with ourselves. Equally, if we want to speak to others in a gentle tone, then we need to learn how to speak to ourselves in that tone too.

When we are self-critical, and berate ourselves internally for the smallest mistake that we make, how can we expect to be able to speak kindly to others? Speaking with a gentle tone comes first when we can learn to speak to ourselves with that same voice.

We need to think before we speak. Our words have more impact than we often realize in the moment, so it's important to pause and take time before we respond. That is hard, because it is easy to react in the moment. Practice the pause. The wisdom we were given as children here is important . . . count to ten.

How we respond will set the tone for the rest of the encounter. As Solomon teaches us:

"A gentle answer turns away wrath,

but a harsh word stirs up anger."[19]

I am sure that most of us know what it is like to be in a difficult conversation. Perhaps it's with a difficult person, or maybe it's just the situation, but sometimes in my head and my heart I can already feel myself getting flustered or defensive. In that moment I have a choice about how I respond. In that moment I need to be sending up a prayer to ask God for the strength to respond gently, because no matter what the situation, I can choose who I want to be. I can't control the other person, or what they think or say, but I can have control over what I think and say. We will touch on this a little more in the next chapter as we look at the fruit of self-control.

Seeking to understand someone else's point of view is helpful when we want to speak in a good tone. Empathy helps gentleness to flourish, so during those pauses, when you're counting to ten, put yourself in the shoes of the other person before you respond.

If we want to be those whose character is shaped like Jesus', then we need not only the fruit of gentleness, but to learn and grow in how we deliver it.

TENDING THE SOIL

What are some of the weeds that can threaten the growth of this fruit in our lives?

Unresolved Anger or Bitterness

We can't control what has happened to us, but we do have the power to respond in a way that keeps our hearts soft.

Lingering anger, resentment, or unforgiveness hardens the heart and chokes out gentleness in our lives.

I remember a pastoral conversation with a man once who really struggled with bitterness. He had suffered a stroke which had left him partially paralyzed down one side of his body. However, this had led to real and deep bitterness within him, which had caused real damage to his family relationships and friendships. The truth is that he wished that he had died, and the fact that he lived with limitations was a reminder to him of what he had lost, rather than what he still had.

---

19. Prov 15:1.

I have not suffered that kind of illness before, and I do not have to live with those limitations. But twenty years ago, I lost my sister to a stroke, and I would have given anything for her to have survived, even with the limitations that this man had.

How we get our minds around major events like that is difficult and takes time, but if we are not careful then the anger we feel can turn into a root of bitterness which will harden our hearts and break our relationships. As the writer of Hebrews reminds us:

> "Keep a sharp eye out for weeds of bitter discontent. A thistle or two gone to seed can ruin a whole garden in no time."[20]

If you are experiencing anger that might be a totally appropriate response to the situation you find yourself in. Don't let that anger be unresolved. Take it to God. Own it in your heart and your mind as what you feel in that moment but don't let it define or consume you. When our anger is unresolved it can lead us down into bitterness, which can cause us to lash out or withdraw rather than respond with Christlike gentleness.

As a church we are exploring the story of Joseph on Sunday mornings, and yesterday I was preaching on Joseph's experience in prison. Joseph had experienced truly terrible times in his young life. He had been bullied, betrayed, sold, enslaved, seduced, and falsely accused. How he found himself in prison. Rather than allow bitterness and unresolved anger to strangle his heart, he leaned into God. He didn't sulk; he served. He allowed his heart to remain soft and open, and so he was able to learn lessons even in this dark and difficult place.

Pain can either soften us or harden us. True gentleness requires a heart that has been softened.

A Harsh or Judgmental Spirit

When we look back at the gentle and humble heart of Jesus in Matthew 11, what we see with a harsh and judgmental spirit is the opposite. Again, there is a hardness to this weed when we are quick to criticize or assume the worst in others. We find it so easy to judge, and we make snap judgements all the time. We judge people by how they look, how they speak, where they are from, as well as countless other criteria. Some of those judgements can be helpful to us and can even protect and keep us safe.

---

20. Heb 12:15, *Message*.

However, judgmentalism comes when we elevate ourselves over another person, abandoning empathy and often labelling them negatively.

This is the spirit of the Pharisees, and it is one that stands in real contrast to the Spirit of Jesus. There are few things that strangle the fruit of gentleness more than judgementalism. Judgement places us in a position above another person.

Think about the story of the woman caught in adultery in John 8.

They bring this woman to Jesus, ready to stone her. They value legalism over love, place themselves as morally superior to her, and condemn her to trick Jesus. Their hearts are hard, and their judgmental spirit stops them from showing gentleness and mercy.

What are the ways that we judge others? Are those judgements justified or are we simply elevating ourselves by putting others down? Are our hearts gentle and humble, or have they become critical and judgmental?

A critical attitude can blind us to the humanity and needs of others, making gentle responses rare.

The Influence of the World's Values

The world often praises aggression, dominance, and assertiveness over gentleness.

Think about the world we live in, especially in the west. When it comes to most work environments; business, education, the media, politics, what people value is ambition, dominance, and assertiveness. Society values and rewards those who go and get what they want, making things happen. They are the people who are labelled *winners*. In most leadership positions many people look for *alpha personalities*, because they feel that this is the type of leader who will get things done. Those who are gentle and humble often get overlooked and discounted as weak or overly sensitive.

Social media often rewards loud opinions or outrage, with people thinking about what sharp comeback they are going to throw out. And because we don't have to look the person in the eye, because the screen we stare at creates a level of detachment and disassociation, we throw gentleness to the wind and say what we want without a filter.

Or think about the television shows or films you watch. Are the main characters gentle and humble, or are they often tough, sarcastic, and dominant? What messages are being communicated to us about the values that are important?

Think about the fast-paced culture we live in. We work like machines and then wonder why we are devoid of empathy? We focus so much on productivity and efficiency that we become cold. We may not have a heart of stone, but at times it can become mechanical, tied to the constant drive of our productivity obsessed culture. It isn't soft anymore. It grinds but doesn't beat.

When our collective conscience is pricked, or our humanity stirred, we often seek to recalibrate the machine to respond more *humanly*. That's not the problem. The problem is not how our behavior looks, but what our heart is. Machines don't have character. They can't. They can mimic behavior, and that's the real challenge when it comes to having the fruit of gentleness in our character. It is not about mimicking Jesus! It is about heart-transformation. As the Lord said to his people through the Prophet Ezekiel:

> "I will give you a new heart and put a new spirit in you; I will remove from you your heart of stone and give you a heart of flesh."[21]

In our fast paced, mechanistic world, we need to slow down, be softer and more present. Our hearts need to change so that they no longer grind along to the pattern and program of our culture but beat to the rhythms of grace and gentleness we see modeled in Jesus.

As we have already explored in this book, Paul warns the Romans not to "become so well-adjusted to your culture that you fit into it without even thinking. Instead, fix your attention on God. You'll be changed from the inside out."

If we want to be gentle, we need a new heart, the heart of Jesus.
Gentleness is the Maker's mark.

QUESTIONS FOR REFLECTION

1. Think of some examples of how Jesus engaged with people in a gentle way?
2. Who in our society or community do we respond to with hardness or judgementalism?
3. Would you describe yourself as having a teachable spirit? What are some of the things you have learned, or ways you have grown recently?

---

21. Ezek 36:26.

4. Would you consider yourself to be a calm presence?
5. What are some of the ways you can apply the golden rule in a spirit of gentleness?
6. Do you struggle with tone? How does it feel to be on the receiving end of someone's harsh tone?
7. Is there any unresolved anger of bitterness that is strangling gentleness in your life?
8. In what ways do you want your heart to be softer?

11

Self-Control

ONCE FOUR PRIESTS WERE spending a couple of days at a cabin. In the evening, they decided to tell each other their biggest temptation. The first priest said, "Well, it's kind of embarrassing, but my big temptation is bad pictures. Once I even bought a copy of the *Sports Illustrated Swimsuit Edition*." "My temptation is worse," said the second priest. "It's gambling. One Saturday instead of preparing my homily I went to the racetrack to bet on the ponies." "Mine is worse still," said the third priest. "I sometimes can't control the urge to drink. One time I actually broke into the sacramental wine." The fourth priest was quiet. "Brothers, I hate to say this," he said, "but my temptation is worst of all. I love to gossip—and if you guys will excuse me, I'd like to make a few phone calls!"

What are your weak spots? What makes you lose control? Think about the start of each year when you make your New Year's resolutions. We approach the start of the new year with such hope and optimism about things we resolve to do less, or to do more. Yet almost half of people give up their resolutions within a month. The problem we have is that the reason we choose them is because we find them hard to master.

In this chapter we are looking at the last fruit of the Spirit: self-control. For many people this is one of the hardest.

If we're honest, we find it hard to say no when we are faced with something we want. When we are tempted to do the thing we want, no matter what the consequences. And if we are honest, even though we live in a world of advertising that plays on our desires and emotions, we know that the hardest person to say no to is yourself.

As we seek to grow in Christ-like character, bearing the Maker's mark, how can we cultivate this fruit in our lives? As we have with all the others, the best place to start is with Jesus.

THE IMAGE OF JESUS

It seems to me that when we look at Jesus, across every aspect of his life and ministry, the term *Master* is an excellent fit. Not simply as a title highlighting his status, but in terms of his approach to everything he did. He sought to master it. That is not about domination, but rather a confidence and security in who he was that allowed him to be in control of his thoughts and actions. There are several examples of Jesus' self-control that can give us encouragement as we seek to be transformed more into his likeness.

Fasting

We have already looked at how Jesus responded to temptation in the wilderness. What highlights how Jesus bore the fruit of self-control is that before that temptation took place, he had been fasting for forty days and nights.

I remember when I was younger, we used to do a sponsored famine to raise money for various charities. In our church youth group, we would go without food for around 24 hours, which hardly constitutes a famine, but when you are a growing teenager certainly seemed significant. We celebrated the end of that sponsored famine like we hadn't eaten in weeks, often with a Chinese take-away.

Fasting is much more than a sponsored hunger strike. It is a spiritual discipline, and it is practiced by people of different faiths and none, all around the world. It was a significant part of Jesus life, and one that he expected to be part of the lives of his followers. We see that when he says during the sermon on the mount, "*when* you fast . . . "[1]

For Jesus, his fast was both Spirit led, and Spirit fueled. Luke tells us that at the beginning of chapter 4 when he tells us that "Jesus, full of the Holy Spirit . . . was led by the Spirit into the wilderness."[2]

---

1. See Matt 6:16.
2. Luke 4:1.

Self-Control

The self-control that we talk about as a fruit of the Spirit is more than self-denial, or extreme will power. It comes through the empowering and leading of the Spirit. It is the fruit born from the life of one who is filled with the Spirit, who bears the Maker's mark.

Anyone who has attempted any type of fast will know that it takes discipline. Bex and I have restarted the discipline of regular fasting, something we used to do regularly until our son was born, and there are times when it is tempting to give in, and when it is hard. That's just after a couple of days. Jesus went without food for forty days, almost six weeks. If you eat three meals a day that's one hundred and twenty meals that he went without! It would have taken tremendous self-control, fueled by the Spirit to accomplish that fast.

The physical cravings that he would have experienced, the tiredness and lack of energy, the loneliness, all increasing over time would have been hourly challenges to overcome. Even writing this makes me feel hungry.

Not only that, having reached the end of his fast, Luke tells us matter-of-factly that Jesus was hungry! When he was at his hungriest, most tired, and most stretched, the tempter came. What was the first temptation?

> "If you are the Son of God, tell this stone to become bread."[3]

It is hard for us to understand how tempting this must have been. After forty days and nights without food, racked with hunger, with nobody watching, the tempter comes presenting himself as one who can meet a need.

Jesus' response is telling:

> "It is written: 'Man shall not live on bread alone.'"[4]

In other words, there are more important things in life than food, and there are more important things in this moment than satisfying my desires. As Dallas Willard reminds us:

> "Fasting confirms our utter dependence upon God by finding in Him a source of sustenance beyond food."[5]

Jesus learned what it meant to submit to God, even when the choice to do so was costly. His ability to take up the cross and be faithful even to death was not a once off extravagant act of self-denial. It was the working out of a life filled with learning what it means to deny himself and be

---

3. Luke 4:3.
4. Luke 4:4.
5. Willard, *Spirit of the Disciplines*, 166.

faithful to the Father. To bear the fruit of self-control. It is an example that he calls us to follow. The invitation is clear:

> "Whoever wants to be my disciple must deny themselves and take up their cross and follow me."[6]

Yes, Jesus invites us to come and experience life in all its fulness. Yes, we are invited as the weary and heavy-laden ones to come and experience rest. However, we are also called in a world of excess and abundance, to experience the Spirit-fueled discipline of self-control. Fasting is a key way we can experience that. Dallas Willard highlights its importance for us as those who seek to be shaped into the image of Jesus:

> "Fasting is one of the more important ways of practicing that self-denial required for *everyone* who would follow Christ."[7]

For Jesus this is key, and for us it is key too. Not for some, but for all. Self-control is not just for those in extreme situations, or for people with a problem. It is for all of us. If you think it's not for you, it is!

As a spiritual discipline it teaches us as trains us to grow in the fruit of self-control, as Jesus did. Richard Foster wrote a great book called *Celebration of Discipline*, in which he looks at the Spiritual disciplines and how they can lead us on a path to growth. He looks at prayer, worship, reading the scriptures, solitude, silence, and service. This is what he says about fasting:

> "More than any other discipline, fasting reveals the things that control us. This is a wonderful benefit to the true disciple who longs to be transformed into the image of Jesus Christ."[8]

We cannot know how to become more self-controlled unless we have an awareness of what in our lives needs to benefit from more control. Fasting, as an act of self-control itself can help us to identify that.

Responsive not reactive

When we look at Jesus, one of his character traits that I think we often don't pay as much attention to, but which would dramatically improve our lives

---

6. Matt 16:24.
7. Willard, *Spirit of the Disciplines*, 167.
8. Foster, *Celebration of Discipline*, 67

SELF-CONTROL

and the lives of those around us is that he was responsive, not reactive. There is a big different between the two.

Being reactive is often immediate, emotional, and often unthinking. It's behavior that is driven by impulse and external pressure. On the other hand, being responsive is thoughtful, intentional, and controlled. It's behavior that is often guided by wisdom and a clear purpose.

Think of how Jesus deals with the constant attempts by the Pharisees to trap him. When the woman caught in the act of adultery is brought to Jesus in John 8, John makes it clear that the intention of the Pharisees was to trap Jesus.[9]

How would you respond to people constantly trying to trap you, trick you and trip you up? If those people followed you around, snidely sniping in from the sidelines of every good thing you were trying to do. The temptation to argue, retaliate, or shut them down with force must have been a very real one. How do you respond to people who become a thorn in your side? Do you respond defensively? Do you lose control? Do you find yourself snapping? We will come to look at these responses in just a moment, but in some ways, we would think of them as perfectly human responses. Yet Jesus, who was fully human, showed great self-control in these moments and instead he answers with questions, parables, or sometimes simply with silence. Rather than losing control and falling into the trap, he always steers the conversation toward the truth of his teaching. He doesn't get baited into arguments but remains composed and focused on his mission.

I read this quote by Oswald Chambers recently in a great book called *Well-Intentioned Dragons*, a book about ministering to problem people in the church:

> "From the Lord's standpoint it does not matter if I am defrauded or not; what does matter is that I do not defraud."[10]

Jesus shows us the way of self-control, that even when he is wrongfully accused, tricked, and trapped, he refuses to respond in kind.

---

9. See John 8:6.
10. Chambers, *My Utmost for His Highest*, 182.

The Maker's Mark

Power Under Control

In the last chapter we looked at the fruit of gentleness as power under control. There is certainly an overlap with the fruit of self-control. There are few places we see that more clearly than in the last 24 hours of Jesus' life.

Our young son Leo reminded me a couple of days ago about the exchange that took place between Jesus and Peter. Jesus had just been betrayed by Judas and arrested, and Peter pulls out a sword to attack one of the guards. Jesus rebukes him, saying:

> "Do you think I cannot call on my Father, and he will at once put at my disposal more than twelve legions of angels? But how then would the Scriptures be fulfilled that say it must happen in this way?"[11]

What control it must have taken to know that in one word seventy-two thousand angels would have descended to save him, and to still choose to be faithful to the Father's plan.

Gethsemane means *olive press*, and it was here beside the Kidron winter stream at the foot of the mount of olives that the olives were crushed under a huge millstone. A wooden screen then presses the broken olives until the pure oil comes out. This was a place of crushing, of pressing, not simply for the olives but on this night for Jesus too. We are told that he was "overwhelmed to the point of death" and that his "sweat was like drops of blood," an extremely rare condition called *Hematidrosis*, where the capillaries around the sweat glands rupture due to extreme stress and fear, causing blood-tinged sweat.

Knowing what is ahead, knowing the power he holds to call a stop to it, and given the mental and physical state he was in, to say *may your will be done* was a staggering act of self-control.

We see it again on the cross. We've already reflected on the patience that Jesus showed to the thief crucified with him, and to those who were taunting him. The self-control it must have taken to take those insults and to not respond. He doesn't curse or condemn but extends grace. Even here he loves his enemies and prays for those who persecute him.

While it might not be the first fruit that comes into our minds when we think of Jesus, it is none the less a significant one, and one that we need to learn from as those who seek to have character shaped like his.

---

11. Matt 26:53–54.

THE FRUIT OF SELF CONTROL

So, as we reflect on this fruit in our own lives, what are the lessons, challenges, and encouragements we can explore?

Sort out your Thought Life

> "Do not conform to the pattern of this world, but *be transformed by the renewing of your mind*. Then you will be able to test and approve what God's will is—his good, pleasing and perfect will."[12]

Craig Groeschel writes:

> "Our lives are always moving in the direction of our strongest thoughts. What we think shapes who we are."[13]

What is it that we spend our time thinking about? What are the thoughts that dominate our lives? Often, we can get fooled into believing a lie and then living as though it's true. How many of us when we have made a mistake or messed up have said "I just can't help it." Is that realty true or is that simply the lie that we have come to believe is true? Because what we believe is true will shape our reality.

This is where transformation is so important. As I have said several times throughout this book, following Jesus is not about behavior modification, but about transformation coming to every area of our lives, and that includes the way that we think. Paul doesn't call us to become *informed*, but to be *transformed*.

What about, instead of believing the lie that you are powerless to change, you believed the truth God gives me power through his Spirit. That is a constant reality throughout the Bible, and it can be the reality of your transformed mind too.

That requires you to take control, to take control of the way that you think. Control doesn't mean that you can't stop certain thought processes or patterns from happening. There are some things that just pop into our thoughts whether we want them to be there or not. But it does mean taking ownership of them.

Paul phrases it like this:

---

12. Rom 12:2.
13. Groeschel, *Winning the War in Your Mind*, 1.

The Maker's Mark

> "We demolish arguments and every pretension that sets itself up against the knowledge of God, and we take captive every thought to make it obedient to Christ."[14]

Did you know that you have more thoughts than you think? A 2020 study found that the average person has around six thousand thoughts per day. That's two hundred and fifty thoughts per hour at just over four per minute. So, what does Paul mean when he says, "take captive *every* thought?" Does he mean all six thousand?

I think what Paul is getting at here is that we need to get to the root of the problem. You see many people spend their time trying to modify or improve their behavior, but the faulty thinking that caused that behavior is still alive and kicking under the surface, running wild in the thoughts that then inform the way a person behaves. Without sorting out your thought life, taking that faulty thinking captive and allowing it to be transformed into obedience to Christ, we cannot hope to live consistently as those who bear the Maker's mark.

Our self-control isn't simply about our actions, but about our thoughts.

Here's a helpful pattern I came across recently.

Firstly, take a thought inventory. It doesn't have to be those six thousand thoughts a day, but the key ones that you have become aware of. What have you been feeling? Have you been happy or sad, joyful or worried? What might have triggered that thinking?

Secondly, start to identify any faulty thinking. What are the thoughts that you have had that aren't true? The measure we can use for this is God's word and allow his voice of truth to speak into our thoughts and help us to see them for what they really are.

Thirdly, hand them over to God. Taking ownership of our thoughts or taking them captive doesn't mean that we must keep hold of them. Having self-control over our thinking doesn't mean hanging onto stuff but putting it in its proper place. Handing it over to God can take a moment, but it's a moment of significance that can transform the way you think.

Fourthly, remind yourself what God's voice of truth is saying. Coming back to the spiritual disciplines that we started this chapter with, we need to be spending time in prayer, reading God's word, fasting, worshipping, so that we can be saturated with the truth God wants us to know, rather than being tossed around by every wind that comes blowing through our minds daily.

---

14. 2 Cor 5:10.

Just Say No

> "So I say, walk by the Spirit, and you will not gratify the desires of the flesh . . . The acts of the flesh are obvious: sexual immorality, impurity and debauchery; idolatry and witchcraft; hatred, discord, jealousy, fits of rage, selfish ambition, dissensions, factions and envy; drunkenness, orgies, and the like. I warn you, as I did before, that those who live like this will not inherit the kingdom of God."[15]

Saying no is not a line in the sand, but its choices every day.

As we look at the list above from Galatians 5, there are some destructive things that Paul categories as acts of the flesh. I don't think by flesh he means that these are things we do in and through our bodies specifically, but that they stand in contrast to the fruit of the Spirit.

As we read down the list there are probably some things most people feel confident aren't an issue for them. Witchcraft? Orgies? For sure that will be an issue for some, but not for many. However, we don't need to spend too much time with the rest of the list until we start to feel a little bit more uncomfortable. Jealousy? Envy? Drunkenness? Fits of rage?

What really struck me was when I read it in the Message translation:

> "It is obvious what kind of life develops out of trying to get your own way all the time: repetitive, loveless, cheap sex; a stinking accumulation of mental and emotional garbage; frenzied and joyless grabs for happiness; trinket gods; magic-show religion; paranoid loneliness; cutthroat competition; all-consuming-yet-never-satisfied wants; a brutal temper; an impotence to love or be loved; divided homes and divided lives; small-minded and lopsided pursuits; the vicious habit of depersonalizing everyone into a rival; uncontrolled and uncontrollable addictions; ugly parodies of community."[16]

You might not be turning up at orgies every Friday night, but how's your temper? Not interested in joining the local coven, that's great, but do you get jealous?

It's important to note that some of the things Paul mentions are part of the nature of a fallen humanity. We cannot be perfect. Does that mean that we should blindly accept that sin is part of our lives and go with it? No, of course not. What it means is that we will never be able, through our

---

15. Gal 5:16, 19–21.
16. Gal 5:19–21, *Message*.

own self-control, to remove all sin from our lives. What we can do, with the Spirit of God empowering us, is seek to say no to sin, and as much as we can, be in control of our own actions.

As I mentioned earlier, now we are looking at the story of Joseph in church. Think about the temptation that Joseph had when Potiphar's wife tried to seduce him. It was not unusual for the master or mistress of a house to behave this way towards slaves. That's exactly what Joseph was. He was not an employee; he didn't have rights or a contract. He did what he was told, when he was told to do it, and the only acceptable answer was to say yes. If the master or mistress said *jump*, you didn't even ask how high, you just did it.

Joseph did two things that can help us as we seek to exercise self-control.

Firstly, in his explanation to Potiphar's wife we see that he understands the consequences of sin:

> "But he refused. 'With me in charge,' he told her, 'my master does not concern himself with anything in the house; everything he owns he has entrusted to my care. No one is greater in this house than I am. My master has withheld nothing from me except you, because you are his wife. How then could I do such a wicked thing and sin against God?'"[17]

What are the consequences of sin? Firstly, it breaks relationships around us. Joseph understands that his relationship with Potiphar would break down if he slept with his wife. His response to this seduction is to reaffirm his faithfulness to Potiphar.

Secondly it damages our relationship with God. Joseph doesn't simply see this as a sin against his master but a sin against God.

Sin breaks relationships.

When sin tries to seduce you, that's the moment to reaffirm your faithfulness! To those around you, and to God.

As we see in the story of Joseph though, sin doesn't just go away! You don't resist temptation once and then that's it, no more temptation for you! Potiphar's wife was relentless, trying to seduce Joseph day after day.

The second thing that Joseph did was to run! He ran away. That's a good strategy for us too. Sometimes you can stand firm in your principles and commitments, but at other times you just need to turn around and run!

I cannot control my temptations, I cannot control other people, I cannot control what happens to me, but what can I control, with God's help? Myself!

17. Gen 39:8–9.

How do we have the strength to do that; to live as those who bear the Maker's mark and have character shaped like Jesus? Paul tells us to walk by the Spirit.

Guard Your Heart

> "Above all else, guard your heart,
>   for everything you do flows from it."[18]

When you squeeze oranges, you will always get orange juice. You won't ever get apple or grape juice! That might seem like an obvious point to make, but it comes down to the simple and yet profound reality, that what is on the inside is what comes out!

We've already looked at this over the course of the book, and it ties in with what Paul was saying a moment ago. If we do not walk in the Spirit, then what is left inside are those sinful desires that then seek to dominate. What comes out then is sinful behavior.

So, the Teacher encourages us in the Proverb to guard our hearts!

That's especially true if we want our hearts to remain soft. Life can throw rocks at us, and so can other people. Over-criticism, rejection, abuse, disappointment, betrayal, lies, judgement, neglect. All these things when they impact our hearts can cause damage, and that can create scar tissue in our hearts that can cause them to become hard.

I came across this beautiful poem recently:

> They threw their words like stones;
> careless, sharp, and sure.
> Some bounced off my skin,
> but some sank deeper than they knew.
> A whisper of betrayal,
> a silence in goodbye,
> the weight of cold indifference,
> a well-aimed, quiet lie.
>
> I gathered them at first,
> thinking strength was stone.
> I built a wall around my chest
> and called that fortress home.

---

18. Prov 4:23.

> Each rock a lesson:
> "Don't trust too soon,"
> "Don't love too wide,"
> "Be careful with your bloom."
>
> But in the night,
> behind that wall,
> I missed the rain,
> I missed it all.
>
> The warmth of being open,
> the wild of letting go,
> the ache of being tender
> in a world that doesn't always show.
>
> So now I sift through rubble,
> stone by heavy stone.
> Some I let dissolve in tears,
> some I leave alone.
>
> For I have learned this truth in full:
> a heart that stays untouched grows cold.
> But one that breaks and beats again
> that heart is forged in gold.[19]

As the poem beautifully highlights, we sometimes guard our hearts with the wrong things. The desire to guard them in response to the call of the Proverb is healthy, but not by creating a wall from the stones that life and people have thrown at us.

Building that wall with the right stones is an act of self-control, of self-care.

When looking at this image of a protective wall, the Teacher also reminds us:

> "Like a city whose walls are broken through is a person who lacks self-control."[20]

When we don't guard our hearts with the truth of God's word then we leave ourselves open to the slings and arrows of outrageous torment, as Shakespeare put it. Guarding your heart through boundaries means being

---

19. *Stones They Threw*, unattributed.
20. Prov 25:28.

intentional about what you let into your mind and emotions. Who comes in? Are they friends or foes? Boundaries that guard our hearts act as a sentinel to let in only what will be good for us: relationships, media, thoughts, environments.

They guard against lies, temptations, or emotional manipulation that can lead to reactive or sinful behavior.

A guarded heart minimizes exposure to influences that trigger impulsive or flesh-driven responses, creating space for Spirit-led decisions.

TENDING THE SOIL

What are some of the weeds that strangle the growth of self-control in our lives?

The Wrong Place at the Wrong time

As I said a moment ago, we can't always know what temptations will come our way, but we can be responsible for how likely temptations are to arise.

It might feel as though we find ourselves simply in the wrong place at the wrong time, but we certainly can put ourselves in harm's way, into places where our self-control is worn down.

Let's look at two examples from scripture.

Firstly, right back at the very beginning. Having placed the first human being, this is the instruction God gives:

> "The Lord God commanded the human, 'You are free to eat from any tree in the garden; but you must not eat from the tree of the knowledge of good and evil, for when you eat from it you will certainly die.'"[21]

At the beginning of the next chapter two Eve is tempted by the serpent, and her response is:

> "God did say, 'You must not eat fruit from the tree that is in the middle of the garden, *and you must not touch it,* or you will die?'"[22]

Here we have an added prohibition that human beings are not allowed to touch the fruit. Scripture gives us no indication that God has added this

21. Gen 2:16–17.
22. Gen 3:3.

stipulation, and it might seem like a small point to make but it will have disastrous consequences almost immediately.

We don't know whether this conversation took place at the tree of the knowledge of good and evil, or if the serpents' words came into her mind the next time she was there. What we do know is that the next recorded action after the conversation with Eve and the serpent takes place at the tree. Was Eve simply in the wrong place at the wrong time? Was she deliberately walking into temptation? We don't know. What we do know is that following that conversation she finds herself by the one tree in all of creation that she was not meant to eat from—and that was dangerous!

What was the problem with the additional prohibition? Eve nervously picks the fruit . . . and nothing happens. No lightning bolt from the heavens. She touched the fruit, and seeing no problem, she continued to eat. Then there is the problem.

We might not have the serpent whispering in our ears directly, but the fierce combination of our own fallen desires and spiritual forces at work in our lives whisper clearly enough to go to places we know we should not go. Then our eyes catch a glimpse of the things we know are not meant for us. We might take a tentative step, waiting for a lightning bolt. When nothing comes, we push further until the boundary is crossed. The damage is done.

And then there is David. In my previous book *After God's Heart*, I looked at David's affair with Bathsheba in a chapter entitled *Balcony Choices*.

> "In the spring, at the time when kings go off to war, David sent Joab out with the king's men and the whole Israelite army. They destroyed the Ammonites and besieged Rabbah. But David remained in Jerusalem.
> One evening David got up from his bed and walked around on the roof of the palace. From the roof he saw a woman bathing. The woman was very beautiful . . ."[23]

David should have been off at war, and because he wasn't where he should have been, he notices Bathsheba bathing on the roof. From there the situation unravels and David commits both adultery and arranges the death of Uriah. All because David was in the wrong place.

Temptation finds us most easily when we're disengaged from what God has called us to do. David should have been leading the army, but instead he was left back in Jerusalem with way too much time of his hands.

---

23. 2 Sam 11:1–2.

As the modern proverb says, "if you don't want to fall, don't walk near the edge."

Addiction

In our church we have multiple recovery programs meeting every day. When you speak with people who go to meetings, they come from all walks of life and come in all shapes and sizes. But there is one thing that they all have in common. Addiction.

Addiction is a very powerful weed that can easily, if left unchecked, strangle self-control in our lives.

Why is addiction so dangerous a threat to self-control? Here are a couple of key reasons.

Addiction Rewires the Brain

Whatever the substance or behavior that you are addicted to, drugs, porn, alcohol, food, screens, when we are exposed to these things for a prolonged period, then the dopamine system in our brains gets overstimulated.

Over time that can become a real issue for us. In our normal and healthily functioning lives and bodies, we experience what are called natural rewards. Peace, joy, fulfilment in relationships. All these things are drowned out by artificial hits of dopamine that we get from the substance we are addicted to.

The cravings we feel then get stronger, and that then links the addictive behavior to feeling good, relief or even survival.

Let me give you an example. Years ago, when I was a much younger adult, I used to smoke. At the age of twenty I had given up and hadn't smoked for six months. When my sister Hannah died, I was standing outside Salisbury hospital, and a passer-by said to me "you look like you could use a smoke." I accepted, felt better and so the link was made in my brain. Whenever I felt sad or stressed, my brain told me that what I needed was to smoke. I smoked the heaviest after that. Praise God that it's now been over ten years since I quit smoking again, but it was a hard thing to do.

When we engage in behaviors that lead to addiction, the brain's impulse control center, called the prefrontal cortex, is weakened. That makes self-control difficult because it makes it harder for us to pause, evaluate, or resist.

Addiction Creates a Cycle of Shame and Despair

Anyone who has suffered with addiction will be familiar with this pattern. You give in to the addiction, and then you feel a sense of guilt, shame and unworthiness because you have failed again. Whenever self-control falters your despair levels go up double. You feel terrible. The awful loop is then that you are caught in this vicious cycle. You feel bad, and so you want comfort, or to numb the pain again and your brain reaches for the one thing that is bound to work; the behavior or substance to which you are addicted. You've created a loop.

That cycle of shame and despair can be a truly dark and isolated place. That's why recovery groups can be a tremendously supportive place. You are not alone. There are people who know what it is like to be where you are.

When your addiction becomes a reflexive coping mechanism, it often bypasses intentional thought. You become reactive to your own cravings rather than responsive to your needs and thoughts.

Addiction Weakens the Will Through Repetition

2 Corinthians 10:4 says:

> "The weapons we fight with are not the weapons of the world. On the contrary, they have divine power to demolish *strongholds*."

A biblical way to think of addiction is to look at it as a *stronghold*, a mental and spiritual fortress that's hard to tear down. We often try to lay siege to it, but the walls have become too strong.

The more a behavior is repeated, the more automatic it becomes. It doesn't take long to make a habit, but it does take a long time to break one, especially the longer it goes on and the behavior is enforced. In this situation self-control is difficult because our will isn't just weak but trained in the opposite direction by our behaviors.

Addiction Clouds Spiritual Sensitivity

Eventually you get to a point where you don't even think you have a problem. As addiction grows, it becomes so ingrained in your life, it's too hard to defeat, that you just stop trying. Your heart becomes numb to conviction. You lose the will to fight. That apathy and shame create a toxic combination

Self-Control

that crowds out time and attention from prayer, reading God's word, and the relationships around you.

People often stop going to church or their support group, because they don't want to be confronted any more with their failure to deal with their addiction. That leads to isolation from the community, which just speeds up all the cycles we have already mentioned.

Self-control is dangerously impacted here, because without spiritual input the Holy Spirit's voice is harder to hear.

The good news is that there is always hope. I have, through God's grace in my life overcome addictions that held me captive and had made my life unmanageable. It took humility, which came in the form of God bringing me to my knees, and it took the love and support of the people closest to me to be loved back to life again, especially Bex. The weapons that Paul talks about can and will demolish strongholds in your life, and I can testify that they have in mine.

What advice can I give you if you are in that place right now? Where you feel as though your self-control has been choked and you feel powerless.

Go along to a meeting. Speak to a loved one. Own what is going on for you and ask for help. Nothing will change unless you admit that there is a problem that needs to be dealt with, and that you are powerless to deal with it on your own.

Keep praying, keep getting on your knees, keep believing the truth of God's word rather than the whispers and lies of the enemy or your own broken thinking.

Don't wait for a better moment, start now!

In ancient Greek mythology, Odysseus had himself tied to the mast of his ship so he wouldn't give in to the Sirens' seductive song. In the face of temptation, he knew that he couldn't trust his feelings or willpower.

Self-control lashes us to the mast by keeping us fastened to God's truth and the character of Jesus, when everything else is screaming to let go and give in.

It's not about stoicism or self-reliance but allowing the Holy Spirit to tie us to something stronger than the storm.

Self-control is the Maker's mark.

THE MAKER'S MARK

QUESTIONS FOR REFLECTION

1. Did you make any resolutions at the start of the year? Have you kept any?
2. Do you fast? What other spiritual disciplines help self-control to grow in your life?
3. Would you say you were a reactive or responsive person?
4. When you must make a difficult choice, do you find it easy to stay in control of your emotions or do they dominate you?
5. Have you ever taken a thought inventory?
6. Are there sins and temptations that you need to run from?
7. Is your heart guarded by the stones that others have thrown at you, or by the truth of God's word?
8. Do you often find yourself in the wrong place like Adam and Eve, and David?
9. Do you struggle with addiction? If so, what help are you getting?

12

A Life of Spirit-Formed Character

As we draw our journey to a close, it's worth pausing to take in the terrain we've traveled.

We began with a simple yet profound truth: that every human being carries the imprint of their Maker. This *mark* is not a mere symbolic stamp, nor is it something to be earned or achieved, but it is an intrinsic part of who we are, placed in us from the very beginning by a loving and intentional Creator. The truth that we are created in the image and likeness of God is not a theological concept for contemplation alone, but a foundation upon which a life can be built; a life shaped into the character of Christ, empowered by the Holy Spirit, and lived in the fullness of love.

What does it mean to live with the Maker's mark visible, not hidden? What does it look like for our daily decisions, reactions, relationships, and priorities to bear witness to the divine fingerprint upon us?

The answer we've explored throughout this book is clear: it looks like Jesus. His life, his attitude, his values, his way of being in the world; his *character*. All of it embodies the kind of human life we are called to live. Jesus is not simply a teacher to admire or an example to imitate. He is the template: Paul reminds us that he is the "firstborn among many."[1] He shows us what it means to be fully human.

And it is not just in moments of worship or quiet contemplation that this shaping occurs. It is in the soil of our everyday lives; in our homes, our

---

1. Rom 8:29.

families, our friendships, our jobs, our struggles and joys that the Spirit is at work, cultivating a character that increasingly reflects the life of Christ.

That fruit we've discussed at length: love, joy, peace, patience, kindness, goodness, faithfulness, gentleness, and self-control. It's not just a list of virtues, or a pick and mix of optional extras, but a portrait of Jesus and the desired outcome of our spiritual formation.

Let's take a moment to reflect on the journey again, fruit by fruit, and consider how these character traits that marked the life of Jesus can become not only our aspiration but our reality.

LOVE: THE ROOT OF ALL FRUIT

We began with love. "God is love,"[2] John writes, and this foundational truth undergirds all that we are called to be. Love is not optional. It is not just one fruit among many. It is the essence of God's being, and therefore the essential character of those who bear his name.

Jesus demonstrated love by stooping to serve, washing the feet of his disciples. He gave love by healing the broken, defending the shamed, welcoming the excluded. And ultimately, he offered love by laying down his life. That kind of sacrificial, servant-hearted love is the fruit we are called to bear. Not love in theory, but in practice.

JOY: A DEEP-ROOTED GLADNESS

Joy, as we discovered, is not mere happiness. It is not rooted in circumstance but in relationship. It is the soul's resonance with the presence of God, even in suffering. When Jesus promised his followers his joy, he wasn't offering fleeting emotion, but enduring strength. In a world that often feels joyless, Christians are to be carriers of celebration: not superficial cheer, but the deep-down conviction that God is good and we are loved.

This joy becomes contagious. It bubbles over in laughter and song, in resilience and gratitude. It transforms suffering into testimony and scarcity into thanksgiving. A joyless Christianity is a contradiction in terms, and a joy-filled follower of Jesus is one who shows the world what the Kingdom of God looks like on earth.

---

2. 1 John 4:8.

PEACE: THE CALM IN THE STORM

In a world fractured by anxiety, conflict, and noise, the peace of God stands out as radically different. Jesus is called the *Prince of Peace*, not because he removed all conflict, but because he brought a deep and reconciling calm into the center of chaos. That peace, shalom, is about wholeness, completeness, and restoration.

When we bear the fruit of peace, we become reconcilers. We listen before we argue. We respond rather than react. We carry calm into the storm, not because the storm isn't real, but because our anchor holds. We've seen that peace grows when we trust God deeply and allow his Spirit to quiet our racing thoughts and settle our hearts.

PATIENCE: THE PACE OF THE KINGDOM

Patience is one of the most misunderstood and undervalued virtues of our day. We live in a culture that prizes speed, instant results, and quick fixes. But God's way is often slower, more deliberate, more like the slow ripening of fruit than the rapid click of a microwave.

Patience isn't passive. It's active trust. It's choosing to wait, not with frustration, but with hope. Jesus was incredibly patient: with his disciples, with the crowds, with his enemies. When we learn to wait on God, to endure with grace, and to withhold judgment, we begin to resemble Christ in deeper ways.

KINDNESS: THE HEART OF GOD ON DISPLAY

In Jesus kindness shines brilliantly. Kindness is love in action, small acts that communicate deep worth. It is more than sentiment; it's practical, courageous, and relational. Jesus didn't just act kindly; he *was and is* kind. His encounters left people restored, not shamed. When we embody this divine kindness in tangible ways, especially toward those overlooked or marginalized, this fruit becomes revolutionary especially in a self-serving world. It reminds us that there is a better way.

GOODNESS: THE GENEROUS HEART

Goodness, as we've seen, is not merely moral decency but a transformative force that blesses others. It is seen in actions that reflect God's justice, mercy, and humility, lived out rather than performed through religious rituals. True goodness stems from a heart shaped by God's Spirit, producing useful and fertile fruit.

The fruit of goodness is grown when we begin to desire the good for others as much as we desire it for ourselves. When we look at Jesus, and his generous character, we see goodness as a lavish, undeserved grace that goes beyond fairness, marked by sacrificial love and extravagant generosity.

FAITHFULNESS: STEADFAST AND SURE

Faithfulness is consistency. It's integrity. It's showing up even when it's hard. God's faithfulness to us never wavers, and we are called to mirror that same trustworthiness in our own lives.

Jesus was faithful to the end. To his mission. To his people. To his Father. He didn't veer off course. And when we allow the Spirit to develop faithfulness in us, we become safe places for others. We become dependable. Not perfect, but steady. We become the kind of people who keep their word, who stay the course, who remain anchored when others drift.

GENTLENESS: POWER UNDER CONTROL

Gentleness is not weakness; its great power restrained for the sake of love. It is great power under great control. In a harsh and abrasive world, gentleness is like balm. Jesus, who had all power, chose to interact with tenderness. With children, with outcasts, with sinners. He was assertive when he needed to be, but never domineering. His was a strength that stooped to lift others up.

When the Spirit develops gentleness in us, we become approachable. Safe. We speak the truth, but we speak it in love. Our tone matters. Our posture matters. Gentleness changes atmospheres. It disarms. It dignifies.

SELF-CONTROL: THE INNER LIFE GOVERNED BY THE SPIRIT

And finally, self-control, the discipline of character. Without this fruit, all the others risk imbalance. Self-control is the Spirit-enabled ability to say no to the things that harm and yes to the things that heal. It is mastery over impulses, habits, and reactions, not for the sake of moral superiority, but for the sake of holiness and freedom.

Jesus exhibited this with stunning clarity. From his forty day fast in the wilderness to the way he endured the cross. He lived aligned with the will of the Father, not with his immediate appetites or emotions. For us to do likewise requires the same Spirit working within.

THIS IS ABOUT TRANSFORMATION, NOT PERFORMANCE

A vital thread that has run through every chapter, and that must be the final word of this book, is that this is not about behavior modification. It is about identity transformation. You do not bear the Maker's mark by trying harder, by ticking spiritual boxes, or by pretending to be something you're not.

Yes, you have a part to play, because the truth is that if you want to have fruit in your life you have to become a gardener. A gardener who helps to tend the soil, help to root out weeds and make sure that the environment you are in remains fertile.

Even though you have a part to play in this process, we must always remember that we bear the Maker's mark because we are his. You are created in his image. You are loved with an everlasting love. And the Spirit who hovered over the waters in creation now hovers over your heart, seeking to bring form to what is formless, and life to what feels dead.

This transformation happens over time. Fruit doesn't appear overnight. There are seasons. There are setbacks. There is pruning. But there is also progress, promise, and presence. God's presence within you, forming you little by little, day by day.

As Paul explains to the Corinthians:

> "We Christians have no veil over our faces; we can be mirrors that brightly reflect the glory of the Lord. And as the Spirit of the Lord works within us, we become more and more like him."[3]

3. 2 Cor 3:18, *Living Bible Translation*.

Performance might act like Jesus; but transformation becomes like Jesus.

THE TREE BY THE STREAM

In Psalm 1, the Psalmist speaks of the person who meditates on God's Word like this:

> "They are like trees along a riverbank bearing luscious fruit each season without fail."[4]

That's the image to carry forward. You are that tree. Planted. Rooted. Nourished. Formed.

Let your roots go deep into the love of Christ. Let your branches reach toward the light of grace. Let the seasons do their work. Some days you will feel fruitful. Other days, you will feel bare. Trust the process. The Gardener is faithful. He does not give up on what He plants.

A healthy tree shows fruit above ground, but the secret is in the hidden root system. The deeper the roots, the more resilient the tree. Spiritual fruit is what others see, but healthy fruit flows from an invisible life with God that we give attention to each day.

What Now? Now it's your turn. This book may be finished, but your journey is not. Keep tending the soil. Keep walking in step with the Spirit. Keep your eyes on Jesus. Stay honest, stay humble, and stay hopeful.

Ask yourself:

How will I reflect the Maker's mark in my day-to-day life?

What fruit is growing in me? What fruit needs more attention?

Where am I resisting the Spirit's gentle pruning?

How can my life, my real, ordinary, messy life, become good soil for transformation?

Let the answers guide you. Let the Spirit lead you. Let the character of Christ become your own. For you, beloved child of God, are marked. You are loved. And you are being made new.

Let that truth shape you, season by season, into someone who shows the world what God is like.

That is the Maker's mark.

---

4. Ps 1:3a, *Living Bible Translation*.

Bibliography

Bridge, Donald. *Travelling Through the Promised Land*. Fern: Christian Focus, 1998.
Card, Michael. *Inexpressible: Hesed and the Mystery of Lovingkindness*. Downers Grove: IVP, 2018.
Chambers, Oswald. *My Utmost for His Highest*. New York: Dodd, Mead and Company, 1935.
Chapman, Gary. *The Five Love Languages: How to Express Heartfelt Commitment to Your Mate*. Chicago: Northfield, 2004.
Comer, John Mark. *Practicing the Way: Be with Jesus, Become like Him, Do as He Did*. London: SPCK, 2024.
———. *The Ruthless Elimination of Hurry*. Colorado Springs: Waterbrook, 2019.
Csinos, David M. and Ivy Beckwith. *Children's Ministry in the Way of Jesus*. Downers Grove, IL: Inter Varsity, 2013.
Dudley Smith, Timothy. *Lord for the Years*.
Eldredge, John. *Beautiful Outlaw: Experiencing the Playful, Disruptive, Extravagant Personality of Jesus*. London: Hodder & Stoughton, 2012.
Fee, Gordon. *Paul, the Spirit and the People of God*. London: Hodder & Stoughton, 1997.
Fennell, Melanie. *Overcoming Low Self-Esteem: A Self Help Guide Using Cognitive Behavioural Techniques*. London: Robinson, 2016.
Foster, Richard. *The Celebration of Discipline: The Path to Spiritual Growth*. London: Hodder & Stoughton, 2005.
Fullerton, W. Y. *I Cannot Tell*.
Giglio, Louis. *Indescribable: 100 Devotions About God and Science*. Nashville: Tommy Nelson, 2017.
Groeschel, Craig. *Winning the War in Your Mind: Change Your Thinking, Change Your Life*. Grand Rapids: Zondervan, 2021.
Hansen, David. *The Art of Pastoring: Ministry Without All the Answers*. Downers Grove, IL: IVP, 2012.
Lewis, C. S. *Letters to Malcom: Chiefly on Prayer*. London: Harvest HBJ, 1964.
———. *Mere Christianity*. New York: MacMillan, 1960.
———. *Surprised by Joy: The Shape of My Early Life*. New York: Harcourt, Brace and World, 1955.
Longman III, Tremper, and D. E. Garland. *The Bible Expositors Commentary: Volume 8*. Grand Rapids: Zondervan, 1984.
Macleod, Donald. *The Person of Christ: Contours of Christian Theology*. Downers Grove, IL: IVP, 1998.

Bibliography

Manning, Brennan. *Abba's Child: The Cry of the Heart for Intimate Belonging.* Colorado Springs: NavPress, 2002.

Manning, Brennan. *The Relentless Tenderness of Jesus.* Grand Rapids, Revell, 2007.

McLaren, Brian. *Naked Spirituality: A Life with God in Twelve Simple Words.* London: Hodder & Stoughton, 2010.

McManus, Erwin Raphael. *The Way of the Warrior: An Ancient Path to Inner Peace.* New York: Waterbrook, 2019.

"Mental Health Facts and Statistics." Mind.org. www.mind.org.uk/information-support/types-of-mental-health-problems/mental-health-facts-and-statistics.

Moffic, Evan. *What Every Christian Needs to Know about the Jewishness of Jesus: A New Way of Seeing the Most Influential Rabbi in History.* Nashville: Abingdon, 2015.

Open Doors. www.opendoors.org/en-US/persecution/countries/.

Ortberg, John. *The Life You've Always Wanted: Spiritual Disciplines for Ordinary People.* Grand Rapids: Zondervan, 1997.

Peterson, Eugene. *The Hallelujah Banquet: How the End of What We Were Reveals Who We Can Be.* Colorado Springs: Waterbrook, 2021.

———. *A Long Obedience in the Same Direction: Discipleship in an Instant Society.* Downers Grove: IVP, 2000.

Piper, John. *A Hunger for God: Desire God Through Fasting and Prayer.* Wheaton, IL: Crossway, 1997.

Sayers, Mark. *A Non-Anxious Presence: How a Changing and Complex World Will Create a Remnant or Renewed Christian Leaders.* Chicago: Moody, 2022.

Schaeffer, Francis. *The Mark of the Christian.* Downers Grove, IL: IVP, 1970.

Stanley Jones, E. *Abundant Living.* Nashville: Abingdon, 1970.

Talmud Bavli, tractate Shabbat 31a

Udanavarga 5:18

Warren, Kay. *Choose Joy: Because Happiness Isn't Enough.* Grand Rapids: Revell, 2012.

Willard, Dallas. *The Scandal of the Kingdom: How the Parables of Jesus Revolutionise Life with God.* Grand Rapids: Zondervan, 2024.

———. *The Spirit of the Disciplines: Understanding How God Changes Lives.* New York: HarperCollins, 1991.

Wright, Christopher J. H. *Cultivating the Fruit of the Spirit: Growing in Christlikeness.* Downers Grove, IL: IVP, 2017.

Yancey, Philip. *What's So Amazing About Grace?* Grand Rapids: Zondervan, 1997.

www.ingramcontent.com/pod-product-compliance
Lightning Source LLC
Chambersburg PA
CBHW062042220426
43662CB00010B/1618